Kisses, Cuddles & Holiday Love

von Bianka Minte-König

PONS GmbH
Stuttgart

PONS

Kisses, Cuddles & Holiday Love

von Bianka Minte-König
Englisch von Emma Bullimore

basierend auf den Geschichten „Summer Downpour & Holiday Amour" und „heiße
Küsse, kalte Füße" von Bianka Minte-König aus den Büchern:

„Summer, Sun & Holiday Love" © 2005
„Schneeflöckchen, Kuss & Kerzenschein" © 2007
by Planet Girl (Thienemann Verlag GmbH) Stuttgart/Wien

Auflage A1   5 4 3 2 1 / 2013 2012 2011 2010

© PONS GmbH, Rotebühlstraße 77, 70178 Stuttgart, 2010
PONS Produktinfos und Shop: www.pons.de
PONS Sprachenportal: www.pons.eu
E-Mail: info@pons.de

Englische Überarbeitung, Annotationen und Übungen: Brian Melican
Redaktion: Canan Özdamar
Logoentwurf: Erwin Poell, Heidelberg
Logoüberarbeitung: Sabine Redlin, Ludwigsburg
Einbandillustration: Birgit Schössow
Einbandgestaltung: Daniel Müller, Stuttgart
Sprecherin/Tonaufnahmen: Nicola Barber, New York
Layout: one pm, Petra Michel, Stuttgart
Satz: Digraf.pl - dtp services
Druck und Bindung: Print Consult GmbH, Oettingenstraße 23, München

Printed in Czech Republic.
ISBN: 978-3-12-010022-5

INHALTSANGABE

Summer Downpour and Holiday Amour

Kiki hat Lust auf Sonne, See und Strand. Nichts Schöneres als Urlaub auf Mallorca. Doch ihre Freunde haben ganz andere Pläne: Eine Erlebnisrad-tour durch Deutschland - ein Albtraum für Sportmuffel Kiki, die nichts als Regen und Blasen voraussehen kann. Trotz allem schwingt sich Kiki auf das Fahrrad, schließlich ist ihr Freund Meik dabei und allein das ver-spricht schon einen romantischen Sommer... trotz Dauerregen und einem schmerzenden Hinterteil und der allzu perfekten Mona, die auch mit von der Partie ist.

Kisses in the Snow

Katie liebt ihre Rituale. Und jetzt hat sie endlich Gelegenheit ihre skep-tischen Freundinnen von der Kraft der weißen Magie zu überzeugen - schließlich sollen sich Vanessa und Kiwi in einander verlieben - ein Paar, das auf den ersten Blick so gar nicht zueinander passt... und nichts könnte dem Glück schneller auf die Sprpnge helfen, als eine magische Liebesspei-se - doch was passiert, wenn sie die falschen Leute essen?

Summer Downpour and Holiday Amour

Kiki

Kiki ist ein Sportmuffel, wie er im Buche steht. Da ist Maniküre doch schon die bessere Alternative. Aber ihren Freundinnen und natürlich auch Meik zuliebe tut Kiki alles und nimmt auch die Strapazen einer Fahrradtour auf sich.

Franzi

Franzi ist die beste Freundin von Kiki und kennt sie sehr gut. Clever wie sie ist, weiß sie ganz genau, dass man Kiki manchmal zu ihrem Glück verhelfen muss und sie weiß auch genau, wie sie Kiki dahin bekommen kann, wo sie sie haben möchte.

Meik

Kikis Freund Meik ist nicht der romantische Typ. Statt Blumen zu schenken oder ein Liebesgedicht zu schreiben, äußert er seine Liebe eher praktisch, zum Beispiel, indem er Kikis Fahrrad repariert. Trotzdem ist seine Liebe stark und aufrichtig.

Kisses in the Snow

Mila

Skifahren macht Spaß und Mila findet es besonders toll. Nicht nur kann sie danach mit ihren Freundinnen heiße Schokolade trinken, sondern auch mit ihrem Freund Markus unter einer Decke knutschen. Für Mila ist die Liebe das allerwichtigste. Die Begeisterung ihrer besten Freundin Katie für Magie kann sie allerdings nicht teilen.

Katie

Katie bleibt immer optimistisch. Sie liebt ihre Freundinnen, glaubt an die Liebe und vor allem glaubt sie an die Magie. Mit der Hilfe der Mondgöttin kann sie alles schaffen. Ihre Mutter unterstützt ihre Zauberei, ihre Freundinnen nehmen sie aber nicht ganz so ernst.

Wie es sich für beste Freundinnen gehört, halten sich die Mädchen stets auf dem Laufenden – natürlich per SMS.

Daher findest Du an einigen Stellen im Text den einen oder anderen „Hilferuf" per SMS.

Dabei gilt es brennende „Love-Questions" zu klären: Wer? Wo? Und vor allem, mit wem?

Beantworte die Fragen. Eine Liste mit SMS-Abkürzungen findest du auf S. 88 und die Lösungen ab S. 122.

Bianka Minte-König

Summer Downpour and Holiday Amour

"Forget it!"

Franzi looks at me in astonishment[1]. "But, Kiki! I thought you'd be the first to say yes!" She looks really disappointed. "What made you think that?"

That's what I want to know. Me and an adventure cycle tour[2]? You must be joking[3]! My bum gets sore after just a short ride to school! And now Franzi has got it into her head[4] that it would be really fun to ride all the way to the North Sea! No way, not with me. And anyway, the North Sea smells like pee!

I want to go to Mallorca! To Alcudia, to Playa Jardin, to see that cute rep[5] from last year. The way he chucked[6] my brother into the swimming pool – that was hilarious[7]! Especially as my brother, the little idiot, couldn't even swim at the time, and we had to make a joint effort[8] to save him. But when we both jumped into the water we bumped[9] heads, leaving me seeing nothing but stars rather than my drowning brother. André, the rep, was obviously tougher than me, but I must have caught him at a very sensitive spot[10], because he sank to the bottom like a stone. I only realised this as the stars slowly started to fade away.

· · · · · · · · ·

1 **in astonishment** – *verwundert*
2 **adventure cycle tour** – *Erlebnis-Radtour*
3 **You must be joking** – *das kann doch wohl nicht dein Ernst sein*
4 **to get into one's head** – *sich in den Kopf setzen*
5 **rep** – *Animateur*
6 **to chuck** – *werfen*
7 **hilarious** – *urkomisch*
8 **joint effort** – *Gemeinschaftsarbeit*
9 **to bump** – hier: *aneinanderstoßen*
10 **sensitive spot** – *empfindliche Stelle*

I was left facing the urgent[1] question: who do I save first? I decided to follow tried and tested[2] wisdom and, as the sayings go, sisters do it for themselves and every man for himself. So I decided to swim to the edge of the pool first to assess the situation[3] properly. And then, if necessary, get help of course! I mean, I couldn't just let my brother and the really cute rep drown! But as I pulled myself out of the pool, a miracle occurred: a small, wet hand grabbed mine – a little Sea God was standing next to me, out of breath[4] in his soaking wet[5] bandana[6], water dripping down[7] his face. My brother, the idiot, had been saved! I grinned at him, deeply relieved. And before I could ask how this miraculous rescue had occurred, he blabbered[8] at me, "I can swim! You won't believe it! I can swim! Underwater too. I came up all by myself and swam over here! Real swimming, with arms and legs, like you taught me…" Great! And good to know. But where was André? I was just about to take a look around when something grabbed my leg underwater. I shrieked, "Urgh, a shark[9], a shark! It's going to eat me…" and as it pulled me underwater, my last words got lost in the waves washing over my head. I tried to make out[10] my attacker underwater. Of course! Back

• • • • • • • • •

1 **urgent** - *dringend*
2 **tried and tested** - *bewährt*
3 **to assess the situation** - *die Situation einschätzen*
4 **out of breath** - *außer Atem*
5 **soaking wet** - *patschnass*
6 **bandana** - *Kopftuch*
7 **to drip down** - *abtropfen*
8 **to blabber** - *plappern*
9 **shark** - *Hai*
10 **to make out** - *herausfinden*

from the dead! It was none other than André pulling another practical joke[1]. The guy just couldn't get enough! I hammered[2] my fist against his broad chest. He grabbed my hand, pulled me towards him and gave me a wet underwater kiss on the lips before we both shot upwards. We reached the surface, panting[3] for breath and laughing.

"You could have killed him!" I gasped.

"Who?"

"My brother! He couldn't swim until just now."

André laughed his deep, bear-like laugh. "And you couldn't kiss underwater until just now, right? But you can learn everything with André! I'm the best rep on the island!"

"Show-off[4]!" I slammed my hand onto the surface of the water and sprayed him in the face.

"Wait there, you cheeky mermaid[5]!" he shouted as I quickly swam off.

Franzi's offended tone of voice[6] wakes me up from my daydream[7], straight out of last year's summer holiday, back to the reality of planning this year's. "I don't understand why you don't want to go. Greetje and Lea are coming. Even Mona's said yes. If we ask Meik and Bastian, they'll probably join us too…" Meik and Bastian. Now

· · · · · · · · · ·
1 **practical joke** – *Schabernack*
2 **to hammer** – *schlagen*
3 **to pant** – *nach Luft schnappen*
4 **show-off** – *Angeber*
5 **mermaid** – *Meerjungfrau*
6 **tone of voice** – *Tonfall*
7 **daydream** – *Tagtraum*

Franzi is really bringing up the big guns[1]. Meik on a cycle tour with Mona while I was away in Mallorca – no way, I wouldn't be able to sleep a wink[2]! "Rubbish! Meik will never ever come with you. He's probably going to France with his mum or dad." I remember that he'd mentioned some holiday home over there and had raved about[3] it.

"Maybe he doesn't want to go there this year."

"Why's that then?"

"Perhaps he'd rather go on the cycle tour with you."

Very flattering[4], but it's hard to believe. Nor do I want to believe it. As much as I like being with Meik, holidays are holidays, and I prefer to spend them under the Spanish sun rather than a drizzly[5] grey sky at home. But I have to admit it: if Meik goes with them I would be taking a big risk. Even if her boyfriend Bastian comes along as well, Mona will always be attractive to guys and who knows how quickly one of them will fall for her. "OK! I'll sort it out with Meik," I say after picturing[6] Meik and Mona on the holiday together. And at the back of my mind, I'm still hoping Meik will come with me to Mallorca… But there's no way he will.

· · · · · · · · ·

1 **to bring up the big guns** - *schwere Geschütze auffahren*
2 **to not be able to sleep a wink** - *kein Auge zumachen*
3 **to rave** - *schwärmen*
4 **flattering** - *schmeichelnd*
5 **drizzly** - *nieselig*
6 **to picture sth.** - *sich etw. vorstellen*

11

"No, Kiki," he refuses as soon as I bring it up. "Mallorca's out of the question¹. I haven't got enough money. Mum wants to redecorate² the flat, so we're on a tight budget³." What a slap in the face⁴! "But a cycle tour isn't free either!" "No, but it's much cheaper than a trip abroad, with flights and everything. I was planning to go on a canoe⁵ tour with the club, but when Franzi told me you really wanted me to go with you, I changed my mind⁶." Meik looks at me affectionately⁷ with his blue puppy dog eyes⁸. "You know I can never turn you down⁹."

I must be going deaf¹⁰. I can't believe what I just heard! How dare Franzi talk Meik into this¹¹ when I hadn't even agreed to go on the bike tour in the first place¹². And I won't ever agree! EVER! Certainly not now. I'm not going to let people blackmail¹³ me. "Come with me to Mallorca!" I try again. "It's much better there. I'll ask Dad if he can lend¹⁴ you the money. I'm sure he will. You can pay him back in instalments¹⁵." I smile. That's a really good idea.

• • • • • • • • •

1 **out of the question** - *es kommt nicht in Frage*
2 **to redecorate** - *renovieren*
3 **to be on a tight budget** - *ein knappes Budget haben*
4 **slap in the face** - *Schlag ins Gesicht*
5 **canoe** - *Kanu*
6 **to change one's mind** - *sich anders entschließen*
7 **affectionately** - *liebevoll*
8 **puppy dog eyes** - *große Augen*
9 **to turn sb. down** - *jdn. abweisen*
10 **to go deaf** - *taub werden*
11 **to talk into** - *überzeugen*
12 **in the first place** - hier: *überhaupt*
13 **to blackmail sb.** - *jdn. erpressen*
14 **to lend** - *ausleihen*
15 **to pay in instalments** - *ratenweise bezahlen*

Meik looks at me glumly[1]. Then he shakes his head. "I know you mean well[2], but I'm not going to get myself into debt[3] just to go on a quick holiday. And certainly not with your dad."

Hmm, I can understand that, but I can't think of anything more amazing than whispering sweet nothings[4] into Meik's ear under the southern sun. But he is so stubborn[5]. Fine! I can be stubborn too. Just watch me! "And there's no way I'm going to spend my summer holidays getting blisters on my bum on some overland pedalo. I want to go swimming, lie about on the beach, and read cheeky books. I have absolutely no desire to break the record for last-man-in-the-cycle-race-with-a-runny-nose[6]-in-the-constantly-pouring-German-rain[7]." I'm quite convinced that, as far as fitness goes, I'll always be behind everyone else. That's right, not everybody can be an Olympic athlete! "Kiki?"

. . . .

1 **glumly** – *mürrisch*
2 **to mean well** – *gute Absichten haben*
3 **debt** – *Schuld*
4 **to whisper sweet nothings** – *turteln*
5 **stubborn** – *hartnäckig*
6 **runny nose** – *Triefnase*
7 **pouring rain** – *strömender Regen*

Oh no! When Meik speaks to me in that voice, negotiations[1] are out of the question. I'm not going to let him twist me around his little finger[2] and sweet talk[3] me into anything.

"Kiki, it'll be great! The whole gang, it'll be fantastic… camping, youth hostels, barbecues and singing… Having fun… and

swimming in the North Sea, sand and I bet you there'll be loads of sun!"

I look up at the grey sky. "Loads of sun? I can't see any at all. Who do you take me for? Yvonne Catterfeld? But I can't move the clouds for you!"

"Wouldn't be such a bad thing," he says with a really cheeky grin. "Kiki, you're just too pessimistic[4]. A rainy June doesn't mean the weather will be bad in August!"

"Oh really? Doesn't it? Are you aware of today's date? Yes, exactly. It's *Siebenschläfer*. And what does that mean? Well come on clever clogs[5]?" Meik looks at me with a strange expression on his face, like he thinks I'm a bit mad. *Siebenschläfer*! Got it? No? Then I'll tell you. When it rains on *Siebenschläfer*, it means it'll rain for the next seven weeks. Got it? And do you know what that means? Exactly! It's going to rain right through our holidays! At least here in Germany!"

· · · · · · · · ·
1 **negotiation** – *Verhandlung*
2 **to twist around your little finger** – *um den kleinen Finger wickeln*
3 **to sweet talk** – *schmeicheln*
4 **pessimistic** – *schwarzseherisch*
5 **clever clogs** – *Schlauberger*

Meik shakes his head in disbelief. "But that's just a superstition[1]."

"No, it's not! It's an old traditional saying. And old traditional sayings are written in my grandmother's hundred year-old calendar which is never wrong."

"Kiki, you're insane!"

"Do you wanna bet?" Meik waves his hand dismissively, but then he seems to be having second thoughts[2]. "OK. Let's make a bet. But you'll have to check the outcome yourself. I bet there won't be a drop of rain on our bike trip. Do we have a bet?"

"Pah! Sure I'll take on the bet. You'll all drown. The cycle paths will be transformed into bottomless bogs[3] that will swallow you up! The way things look today, it will rain at least as much as it did the last time we had summer floods. But, fine, if you really want to bet."

Meik grins mischievously[4]. "OK. Deal. The bet's on, and you're coming with us to check it out!" He'd got me hook, line and sinker[5], the sneak[6]!

• • • • • • • • •

1 **superstition** – *Aberglaube*
2 **to have second thoughts** – *sich etw. anders überlegen*
3 **bog** – *Sumpf*
4 **mischievously** – *verschmitzt*
5 **to fall for sth hook, line and sinker** – *voll auf etw. hereinfallen*
6 **sneak** – *Schleicher*

"Never! I'm going to fly my backside over to Spain's sunny beaches by plane, not torture it on some rock-hard[1] bicycle saddle[2]. And neither your sweet talking nor your crafty[3] bets can stop me. And that's the end of that!"

TR. 02 When I get home, I start having second thoughts too. What am I doing? I'm not usually as cold and uptight[4] as that. My period[5] must be on its way. That sometimes makes me really unbearable[6]. Good old hormones! What a pain! The basic idea of a cycle tour is really great, and now I am annoyed with myself for blowing my chances[7] of going with them. There's no way I can change my mind now. I still have my pride. It's a shame I've missed the boat[8]! Then the tables turn, not because of my late realisation, or Meik's trick, or Franzi's powers of persuasion[9], but because my aunt Sophia gives birth to her fourth child very prematurely[10], and Mum wants to rush off to southern Germany with

```
Love-Question 1
☑ INBOX
from: Meik Mobile

Hey hun, are you
still in a mood with
me about the hols?
:-( M x
```

· · · · · · · · ·

1 **rock-hard** – *steinhart*
2 **saddle** – *Sattel*
3 **crafty** – *schlau*
4 **uptight** – *verklemmt*
5 **period** – *Menstruation*
6 **unbearable** – *unerträglich*
7 **to blow your chances** – *sich die Gelegenheit entgehen lassen*
8 **to miss the boat** – *eine Gelegenheit verpassen*
9 **powers of persuasion** – *die Überzeugungskraft*
10 **prematurely** – *frühzeitig*

my idiot brother to look after my various young cous- ins while Auntie Sophia takes care of little Linda at the hospital. "It's the least I can do[1] for my sister in this situ- ation." Mum throws herself into her Mother Teresa role wholeheartedly[2] and ignores my arguments. "But I need a Mallorca holiday!" I whine[3], full of self-pity[4]. "I can't live without sun! I get depressed. I wilt[5] like a flower without light."

"Don't talk nonsense. We Germans get by perfectly well with our weather conditions without having to wilt. Or do you think I look wilted?" I think it's best to keep my mouth shut. "I thought you wanted to go on a bike trip with your class this year? Franzi's mother asked me what I thought of the idea at parents' evening[6]." Oh no! Not her as well. Why do our mothers have to poke their noses in[7]? "I thought it was a great idea, but we'd have to make sure that an adult accompanied[8] the group one way or another…"

Huh? An adult accompanying us? Well, great. If I had in- deed, in my moments of weakness[9], thought about going with them, my mother's stipulation[10] takes these thoughts out of my mind. Besides, I'm old enough to know what's

. . . .

1 **the least I can do** – *das Geringste das ich tun kann*
2 **wholeheartedly** - *ernsthaft*
3 **to whine** – *jammern*
4 **self-pity** – *Selbstmitleid*
5 **to wilt** – *verwelken*
6 **parents' evening** – *Elternabend*
7 **to poke one's nose in** – *seine Nase hineinstecken*
8 **to accompany** – *begleiten*
9 **moment of weakness** – *Anflug von Schwäche*
10 **stipulation** - *Bedingung*

17

good for me, and that's anything but a silly bike trip through stupid, wet, northern Germany.

"Then I'll just stay at home on my own and sit in front of the TV," I sigh with some resignation[1]. Mum's not happy with this idea.

"You certainly won't be doing that, my dear," she says a little too kindly. "If you don't want to go away with your friends – not that I understand why you don't– then you can come and help me look after Auntie Sophia's children."

"No way! That's pure blackmail! Forced labour[2]! That's… that's illegal[3] under the Protection of Young Persons Act! Even children have the right to go on holiday!" It's really nice of her to be there for her sister, and normally I might have gone and helped her out, but I've really slogged my guts out[4] in school this year and I just have to have a break. I can't handle loads of screaming little kids. No, I can't do that to Mum – running around her like a bundle of nerves[5] while she's stressed out. I'm doing that enough at the moment. I have an idea. "I can go and stay with Dad in Berlin." My dad is a Member of Parliament[6], and he has a small apartment near Alex. There's always a lot going on around there in the summer. Gay festivals, pop concerts, lots of fun and stuff to do. I'm over the moon[7] with the idea. That's just what I will do. Cycle tour? Forget

· · · · · · · · ·

1 **with some resignation** - *resigniert*
2 **forced labour** - *Zwangsarbeit*
3 **illegal** - *gesetzwidrig*
4 **to slog your guts out** - *schwer arbeiten*
5 **bundle of nerves** - *Nervenbündel*
6 **Member of Parliament** - *Parlamentsabgeordneter*
7 **over the moon** - *überglücklich*

it! But Mum throws a spanner in the works[1] again. "Your father is with a delegation[2] in China, you know that perfectly well. You don't actually think I'd let you hang out in Berlin on your own, do you?"

"No?"

"No, certainly not! And there's nothing you can do about it." As is always the case with us, things go back and forth[3] for a while. I get all worked up, and Mum's patience eventually runs out.

"Now that's enough!" she exclaims, exasperated[4]. "Bike trip or southern Germany! Think about it. Those are your choices."

I rush out of the kitchen to my room and slam the door shut behind me. Mum should know I'm angry, even if a part of me can understand why she doesn't want me staying at home on my own or hanging out in Berlin. But it's still nasty of her to put me under such pressure[5].

I throw myself onto my bed, grab my mobile and call Franzi. "It's all your mum's fault," I bark[6] down the phone.

"Huh? Why's it her fault?"

"She talked my mum into making me go on the bike trip with you!"

· · · · · · · · ·

1 **to throw a spanner in the works** – *Sand ins Getriebe streuen*
2 **delegation** - *Delegation*
3 **back and forth** – *hin und her*
4 **exasperated** – *verärgert*
5 **pressure** – *Druck*
6 **to bark** - *anbellen*

"Really? That surprises me." Franzi is clearly playing the innocent. "I've no idea how she came up with that."

"Oh no?"

"What does your mum think about the idea?"

"Stupid question! Why don't you ask me what I think about the idea?"

"OK. What do you think?"

"I'm not allowed to think anything! I'm being blackmailed." Did I just hear a stifled[1] giggle on the other end of the line? "And what form does this blackmail take?" "Babysitting, looking after screaming children, washing pots and pans, peeling potatoes[2] – in a nutshell[3]: forced labour for my aunt's little brats[4] – or a bike trip with you." Now the laughter is unmistakable[5]. Franzi can't contain it any longer.

"And so you're going with the little brats?" she says, bursting out laughing.

I hold the phone away from my ear, and when she calms down[6], I hiss[7], "Exactly. And I hope you have a nice time!" Then I hang up[8]. That'll give her something to think about! A few seconds later my mobile starts ringing. It's Franzi of course, utterly beside herself[9].

• • • • • • • • •

1 **stifled** – *erstickt*
2 **to peel potatoes** – *Kartoffeln schälen*
3 **in a nutshell** – *kurz gesagt*
4 **brat** – *Balg*
5 **unmistakable** – *unverwechselbar*
6 **to calm down** – *sich beruhigen*
7 **to hiss** – *anzischen*
8 **to hang up** – *auflegen*
9 **to be beside oneself** – *ganz aus dem Häuschen sein*

"You don't seriously mean that, do you? You can't possibly prefer idiots like that to us!"

"Can't I?"

"No!" Now it's my turn to laugh. "Don't worry, I don't! Do you think I'm a freak, or something? I'd rather go with you!" This time I hang up the phone on an overjoyed [1] Franzi.

"Great! I have to tell Greetje and Lea straightaway! This means the Pepper Dolls are all together!"

The Pepper Dolls – that's our girls' club, and if all of us go on the trip together, it's bound [2] to be a party.

Franzi isn't the only one with calls to make. There's someone I have to tell the good news to. What will Meik think of my change of tune [3]? Will he still be angry?

"Meik?"

"Yeah, Kiki? What's up?"

> Love-Question 2
> ☑ INBOX
> from: Franzi Mobile
>
> Kiki, it's so cool that ur coming cy-cling with us! This holiday is gonna rock! :-) xxx

"I've got some news. I think I will check out the bet myself and… come with you." Hearing Meik so over the moon sends a tingle [4] of excitement down my spine. As I hang up and put the phone down next to my bed, I can't help

· · · · · · · · ·

1 **overjoyed** – überglücklich
2 **bound to be** – werden müssen
3 **change of tune** – Kehrtwendung
4 **tingle** – das Prickeln

smiling to myself at the thought of the trip. If, at that moment, I'd had even the faintest idea[1] of what I was letting myself in for, then I would have gone on my knees to my mother and begged[2] her to please, please take me with her to my aunt's stinky-bummed brats!

TR. 03 ⊙ The first day begins with the loveliest drizzle. At the same time Mallorca is experiencing a serious heat-wave[3]. Great! I might well win the bet with Meik hands down[4], but for what? A pair of wet feet! We meet at the station because we are planning to do the first leg[5] to the moor[6] by train. We already checked in our bikes the day before. They'll be waiting for us when we reach our first destination. Mum's not exactly in the best of moods as she drives me to the meeting point with my rucksack and sleeping bag. All at some unearthly hour[7] of the morning, of course. Maybe I really should have gone for the alternative of spoiled brats down South? When I get to the station, I feel like the rug has been pulled out from under me[8]. Franzi is dragging[9] everyone she knows along on this cycling tour. It looks worryingly like a school trip. It's not just Mona who gets on my nerves[10] straight

· · · · · · · · ·
1 **to not have the faintest idea** – *keine blasse Ahnung haben*
2 **to beg** – *bitten*
3 **heatwave** – *Hitzewelle*
4 **to win hands down** – *mit links gewinnen*
5 **first leg** – *erste Etappe*
6 **moor** – *Heide*
7 **at some unearthly hour** – *in aller Herrgottsfrühe*
8 **to pull the rug from under you** – *jdm. den Boden unter den Füßen wegziehen*
9 **to drag along** – *jdn. mitreißen*
10 **to get on your nerves** – *nerven*

away, standing there arm in arm[1] with Bastian while talking to Meik, but the rest of the boys, too. For God's sake, does Franzi have to bring Raffi along? And I don't really know much about Lea's latest boyfriend, Torsten. Now all we need is for Greetje to drag along some guy. And that's just what she does! My chin hits the ground as I see her father, our art teacher, a.k.a.[2] van Gogh, turn up. And if my eyes aren't deceiving[3] me, he's pushing along a Dutch lady's bicycle as well. It soon becomes clear that he's our adult chaperone[4]. "I think I'm going to faint!" is the first thing that comes into my head. He is the last person I would have thought of for a sporty trip like this.

"Well, you know…," he says a bit bashfully[5] after saying hello, "… Greetje begged me to come along so the whole trip wouldn't be cancelled. She got down on her knees, so here I am. Is that OK with you?"

"Sure," Franzi and I say in unison. Van Gogh is alright really. He is one of the few teachers who hasn't completely forgotten what it's like to be young.

• • • • • • • • •

1 **arm in arm** - *eingehakt*
2 **a.k.a.** - *auch bekannt als*
3 **to deceive** - *täuschen*
4 **chaperone** - *Begleiter*
5 **bashful** - *schüchtern*

I look at Mona out of the corner of my eye[1] and wonder what she's chatting to Meik about. He is hanging on her every word[2] and doesn't even notice me arriving. If this is what it's like at the beginning, I wish I'd stayed at home! Look, just to make it perfectly clear: I've got nothing against Mona. Honest. It's just that she's – how can I put it? – she's got the kind of personality that makes a girl get edgy[3] when she's around boys, let alone[4] your own boyfriend. From the moment she turned up in my class with her long hair, her perfect figure and her easy-going attitude she had a hypnotic effect on the boys. They follow her like puppies, helplessly caught under her spell[5]. And the most stupid thing is that there's nothing she can do about it. She goes through life being the picture of innocence[6], driving me up the wall[7]. Inside. But I don't let it show on the outside. Besides, she's always very friendly and funny. But, nonetheless, my blood starts boiling as I see the way Meik is clinging to her. Fortunately, before I explode, Meik finally notices me.

"Kiki!" he calls over to me with what I think is false enthusiasm[8], and takes a few large steps towards me, before he takes my rucksack off my back. "Give that to me. Wow, that's heavy! What have you packed? Stones?"

· · · · · · · · ·

1 **out of the corner of my eye** – *aus dem Augenwinkel*
2 **hang on every word** – *am jmds Lippen hängen*
3 **edgy** – *nervös*
4 **let alone** – *geschweige denn*
5 **under her spell** – *verhext*
6 **innocence** – *Unschuld*
7 **to drive sb. up the wall** – *jdm. auf den Wecker fallen*
8 **false enthusiasm** – *falsche Begeisterung*

"It's a perfectly normal rucksack, not the big, bad wolf!"
Does he think I'm some old nanny-goat who fills up
wolves' stomachs with stones or something? He's going
a bit over the top [1]! I'm not really into compliments like
that. Things could get tense [2] around here! I glance [3] over at
Mona. Why does her boyfriend have his arm around her
while mine is just telling me Grimm fairytales? Just then
the train comes roaring into the station - thank God - and
the next thing on the agenda [4] is to divide ourselves up
into the various compartments [5]. Needless to say [6], Meik
immediately dumps [7] his gear next to Bastian, and I have
Mona on my heels [8] whether I want her there or not. I
drop down into my seat with a sigh and stare at her. One
thing's for sure: if this trip isn't going to turn into a complete nightmare, I'm going to have to change how I feel
about her. Maybe she could teach me something. I really
like the way she's so relaxed with Bastian… I can't help
grinning as I come up with a great idea. I'm going to copy
Mona! Exactly! Like a clone [9]. Everything she does with
Bastian, I'll do with Meik. It would be really bad if I didn't
have the same effect on my boyfriend as she does on hers.
As soon as Meik sits down next to me, I try it out: I grab

· · · · · · · · ·

1 **over the top** – *übertrieben*
2 **tense** – *angespannt*
3 **to glance** – *blicken*
4 **agenda** – *Programm*
5 **compartment** – *Abteil*
6 **needless to say** – *natürlich*
7 **to dump** – *abladen*
8 **to be on one's heels** – *jdm. dicht auf den Fersen sein*
9 **clone** – *Klon*

his arm and put it around my shoulder. Nice and cuddly!
But instead of putting his arm around me properly, like
Bastian does with Mona, he pulls it back and says,
"Do you fancy a sandwich as well? I'm really hungry. I
didn't even have any breakfast."
Well then! Bon appétit. While he eats, I look out of the
compartment window – at the rain.

We've been on the move[1] for some time when the ticket
collector[2] comes along. There's trouble straight away. Van
Gogh decided to be our chaperone pretty late in the day[3].
Although he has a ticket for himself and one for his bike,
he hasn't reserved a place in the transport carriage for his
bike.
"It's not such a big deal[4]," he says to the ticket collector.
"It's perfectly alright in the aisle[5]."
"You're not in a position to judge that," disagrees the woman sternly[6]. "The aisle is not a storage space[7]. Your bike is
blocking people's passage."
Van Gogh starts to get a bit irritable[8]. "What do you sug-
gest I do?"

• • • • • • • • •
1 **to be on the move** - hier: *unterwegs*
2 **ticket collector** – *Zugbegleiter*
3 **late in the day** - *spät*
4 **big deal** - *ein großes Geschäft*
5 **aisle** - *Gang*
6 **sternly** – *ernst*
7 **storage space** - *Laderaum*
8 **irritable** - *gereizt*

"Get out at the next station and make a reservation. The storage spaces for bicycles are all occupied on this train. And without a reservation you have no right to have your bike transported."

We can't believe it, but there is nothing else we can do. At the next station the ticket collector waves over one of the railway attendants and, before van Gogh knows it or we can do anything about it, they dump his bike onto the platform.

"What am I supposed to do now?" cries van Gogh in utter dismay[1]. As a Dutchman, the whole thing must be completely incomprehensible[2] to him. It's just another example of German bureaucracy[3].

"You'd better get out," advises Bastian. "Otherwise you might never see your bike again."

This seems like the best solution to all of us, so we hand van Gogh his rucksack, with all his papers inside, and leave him behind with his bike. We won't be seeing him again any time soon. We've just picked up our bikes at our destination when van Gogh calls us. The next available bicycle storage space on a north-bound train is in two days time. That's too long. If we wait for him, we'll miss the ferry to the island of Wangerooge. And it's almost as

· · · · · · · · ·

1 **utter dismay** – *völlige Bestürzung*
2 **incomprehensible** – *unbegreiflich*
3 **bureaucracy** – *Bürokratie*

impossible to get tickets for another ferry at this time of year as it is to transport a bicycle by train. We curse¹ German Rail.

"What are we going to do now?" whimpers² Greetje. "Without adult supervision?"

Bastian and Meik chuckle³. "Well, if you ask me," says Meik, "we should start the cycle tour on our own. After all, Bastian and I both have youth leader certificates⁴. Van Gogh can try to catch us up."

No sooner said than done. Bastian gets on the phone and settles⁵ things with Greetje's dad. Our chaperone takes a note of all our daily destinations and promises to catch up with us as soon as possible. However he can. It's a good thing he can always reach us by mobile.

 TR. 04 Although it's hard to believe after all the to-ing and fro-ing, later we do actually find ourselves heading northwards on a narrow cycle path alongside a country road. Northwards towards the land where the sheep watch over the dykes⁶ and baa⁷ when they flood – or something like that. Or is it geese⁸ that cackle⁹ when danger is near? Whatever. It's probably all three: sheep,

· · · · · · · · ·
1 **to curse** - *verfluchen*
2 **to whimper** - *wimmern*
3 **to chuckle** - *glucksen*
4 **certificate** - *Bescheinigung*
5 **to settle** - *abmachen*
6 **dyke** - *Deich*
7 **to baa** - *blöken*
8 **Geese** - *Gänse*
9 **to cackle** - *gackern*

geese and – if it carries on raining like this – floods as well. We put on our raincoats, wrap our rucksacks and baskets in plastic, and fearlessly set off on our tour, scoffing[1] at the threat of catching a cold[2]. Our destination: the beautiful island of Wangerooge, which, according to Franzi and Meik's calculations, will take three days to reach. I just want to see if I survive the first! Meik, Franzi and Bastian are acting like experts, looking at the map and explaining the route. They lead us through a tourist area, which is well worth seeing. Yes, well… it would be worth seeing if we could make it out from behind the wall of rain.

As we head into one of the local villages and cycle round a sharp bend[3], a huge carthorse[4] suddenly gallops out of a field towards me. I slam on the brakes[5] and skid[6] past the huge creature's tail with screeching tyres[7]. The horse brays[8] and – as if it has just been called – a tiny steed[9] shoots out of the same meadow and immediately clings to the hooves[10] of the carthorse.

• • • • • • • •

1 **to scoff** – *über etw. spotten*
2 **to catch a cold** – *sich erkälten*
3 **sharp bend** - *Knick*
4 **carthorse** - *Kaltblut*
5 **to slam on the brakes** - *plötzlich heftig bremsen*
6 **to skid** - *gleiten*
7 **screeching tyres** - *kreischende Reifen*
8 **to bray** - *wiehern*
9 **steed** - *Ross*
10 **hoof** - *Huf*

"A pony! What a sweet pony!" cries stupid Lea straight away[1] - she loves horses. "Shall we try to catch it?"

"Sure," I reply dryly – as far as you can be dry in the pouring rain. "Ask Meik where he packed the lasso." Mona hurries over and laughs at my joke, while Lea just looks at me confused. We cycle on while the two stray[2] horses trot[3] along in front of us down the main road of the village. We don't dare try to overtake them, so we just stay at a safe distance. I keep thinking that a car might shoot out from behind the next corner any minute and sweep the two horses off the road.

Mona, who seems to be thinking the same thing, says, "One of us has to do something!" and pedals[4] at high speed to catch up with the horses. I copy her, though I ride alongside the pony while she's next to the carthorse. She calls something out several times, and eventually the carthorse stops in its tracks[5]. What on earth[6] was the magic word[7]?

"Brrrrrrrrrrrrrr!" I call into the pony's ear from behind. It shakes its head sharply, kicks its legs and runs sideways into the driveway of a detached house.

· · · · · · · · ·

1 **straight away** - *sofort*
2 **stray** - *streunend*
3 **to trot** - *traben*
4 **to pedal** - *strampeln*
5 **to stop in your tracks** - *aufhalten*
6 **what on earth?** - *Was in aller Welt?*
7 **magic word** - *Zauberwort*

Someone opens a window. "Hey, get your pony off my property[1]!" a typical housewife shouts at me.

"That's not my pony!" I growl[2] back at her.

"So why are you scaring the poor animal like that?"

"The poor animal scared me, not the other way around."

"Horses are very sensitive. You don't shout in their ears!" she nags[3] at full volume[4].

"I'm very sensitive, too, when people do that to me!" I hiss back at her. In the meantime the others have gathered around me, and Mona does the most annoying thing. She comes sauntering[5] around the corner with the run-away carthorse in tow[6], leading it by its bridle[7] like a placid[8] lap-dog[9]. A flash of recognition[10] lights up the face of the country bumpkin[11].

"That's farmer Jürgens' young Else. So that must be Fidelius." She turns around and shouts back into the house, "Svantje, Fidelius is wandering around the garden. Get out here and ride him over to farmer Jürgens." And then she turns back to us and, in a slight more friendly tone, inquires if there's, "Anything else?"

. . . .
1 **property** – hier: *Grundstück*
2 **to growl** – *knurren*
3 **to nag** – *nörgeln*
4 **at full volume** – *in voller Lautstärke*
5 **to saunter** – *schlendern*
6 **in tow** – *im Schlepptau*
7 **bridle** – *Trense*
8 **placid** – *gelassen*
9 **lap-dog** – *Schoßhund*
10 **recognition** – *Erkennung*
11 **country bumpkin** – *Landei*

Mona and I look at each other.

"No," says Mona. "Just this once we won't charge you anything for catching them, but if Else and Fidelius keep doing this, the horse butcher[1] will probably get called in soon. They can't always get lucky with oncoming traffic[2]!"

"Horse butcher!" An eight-year-old country kid with fair hair and freckles[3] snaps at us. "There aren't any horse butchers around here! We ride horses, we don't eat them!"

"Nor do we," says Mona timidly. "I was just trying to say it's dangerous for them if they get hit by a car…"

"Cars don't do that around here. They know horses roam freely[4]."

Oh, well, in that case… I grab my bike and get back on. I prefer it to riding a live creature like these two horses.

Mona looks uncertainly between us and the carthorse.

"And what shall I do with him now?"

"Give him a slap[5] on the bum and send him home."

Mona slaps him on his behind, and Else strolls off calmly, following the pony.

"For God's sake!" I groan as I imagine what would have happened if I hadn't braked quickly enough and had crashed[6] into the carthorse from the side.

. . . .

1 **butcher** – *Fleischer*
2 **oncoming traffic** – *entgegenkommender Verkehr*
3 **freckles** – *Sommersprossen*
4 **to roam freely** – *sich frei bewegen*
5 **to slap** – *jdn. ohrfeigen*
6 **to crash** – *krachen*

"Forget about it," says Franzi before the full horror of the scenario unfolds[1] in my mind. "There won't be horse stew[2] today!"

"But now you mention it," says Raffi, "eating wouldn't be a bad idea."
So we decide to ride on for a bit until we find an affordable place to eat, which we do. We peel off[3] our rain clothes and throw them onto the traditional pub benches. There's a hearty[4] sausage stew on the menu and, after the landlord reassures[5] us that the sausages definitely aren't made from horses involved in road accidents, we tuck in[6]. After eating we get back on our bikes, and soon my bum starts aching[7], just as I had expected. I can't help thinking about a nice cushion tied to my backside. That would be nice. Bicycle saddles are far too hard for my delicate physique[8]! Unfortunately the fine drizzle doesn't go away, and at dusk a mist rises from the fields and merges[9] with it to form a white wall.

· · · · · · · · ·

1 **to unfold** – *sich entfalten*
2 **stew** – *Eintopf*
3 **to peel off** – *abziehen*
4 **hearty** – *herzhaft*
5 **to reassure sb.** – *jdn. beruhigen*
6 **to tuck in** – *reinhauen*
7 **to ache** – *schmerzen*
8 **delicate physique** – *zierliche Figur*
9 **to merge** – *verschmelzen*

"Lets look for a bed and breakfast," insists Lea, who's also had enough[1] by now.

But Meik says we only have a few more kilometres to go until we come to a farmer who lets people stay in his barn[2] for free. He'd found this out from an alternative travel guide for nature lovers and eco-freaks. "We can get fresh milk there and make ourselves cosy."

That's what I said. Probably some eco-farmer. It's already dark when we get to the farmhouse which is situated somewhat off the beaten track[3]. The barn is empty, and the farmer is rather baffled[4] that we don't want his cosy guestrooms, but want to sleep in the cold barn instead. I mean, if anyone asked me... But no one did. So we take up quarters[5] like the finest soldiers of the German army. We hang out our soaked clothes over the farm machinery[6] to dry and climb up a wobbly ladder onto the barn's upper level, which is filled with hay. After a major hay fight we lay out our sleeping bags for the night. I'm completely exhausted[7] by the time I slip into my sleeping bag and happen to glance over at Mona lying in Bastian's arms. Grrr. Envy[8] creeps up in me. Why is Meik so complicated? Couldn't he just sit next to me and give me a loving hug as

· · · · · · · · ·

1 **to have enough** - *die Nase voll haben*
2 **barn** - *Scheune*
3 **off the beaten track** - *weit ab vom Schuss*
4 **baffled** - *verwirrt*
5 **quarters** - *Unterkunft*
6 **farm machinery** - *Landmaschinen*
7 **exhausted** - *erschöpft*
8 **envy** - *Neid*

well? No, he has to spread out the map and plan the route for the following day. I'm in even more of a bad mood as I watch Franzi cuddling up with Raffi and Lea snogging[1] Torsten.

"It's absolutely freezing," I say in the hope of getting a cuddle[2].

"You're right," says Meik. "It is pretty cold for this time of year. There's usually twelve hours of sunshine around here in August and an average temperature of twenty-eight degrees."

"Oh, really?" Not the result I wanted! I don't want to hear the weather forecast, I want him to move a bit closer, take me in his arms and give me some body heat[3]. No chance!

"OK, people!" Meik eventually calls out as he packs away his map. "Let's go to sleep!" After glancing at Mona and Bastian, he adds a word of warning[4], "Everybody in their own sleeping bag. Don't forget we promised van Gogh we wouldn't let him down[5]."

Bastian and Mona giggle. "But we're not."

Franzi comes over to me with Raffi.

"Really! The way Mona throws herself at Bastian!" says Franzi disapprovingly[6]. "It's totally inappropriate[7]. I'm glad Meik warned them. I wouldn't be surprised if she

· · · · · · · · ·

1 **to snog** – *knutschen*
2 **cuddle** – *Umarmung*
3 **body heat** – *Körperwärme*
4 **to give sb. a word of warning** – *jdn. abmahnen*
5 **to let sb. down** – *jdn. enttäuschen*
6 **disapprovingly** – *missbilligend*
7 **inappropriate** – *ungeeignet*

sneaks¹ into Bastian's sleeping bag with him!"

I can't help thinking, "What would be wrong with that?" And, without thinking about it, that's just what I say to Franzi.

"Well, I prefer to sleep in my own sleeping bag," says Franzi. "You, too, I guess?" She looks at me for solidarity. She makes it quite clear that sharing sleeping bags isn't her thing, and to be honest² it's not mine either. So I'm quite pleased about Meik's announcement³.

He looks at his watch. "It's ten thirty. If we really want to set off early in the morning…" Then he gives me a goodnight kiss and slips off like a good boy, an example to the others, into his one-person sleeping bag. Raffi hits the sack⁴ too. We Pepper Dolls settle down⁵ in the hay in the corner, before Mona comes over to join us. So much for sneaking off into Bastian's sleeping bag! She isn't as stupid as Franzi thinks. I'm freezing cold. What a crap summer! After we've finished bedding down, I glance over to Mona's sleeping bag. There's no sign of movement. On the other side of the room Bastian sounds like he's sawing up half a forest with his snoring⁶. Then I cuddle up into my sleeping bag and fall asleep, my mind at rest.

• • • • • • • • •

1 **to sneak** – *schleichen*
2 **to be honest** – *ehrlich gesagt*
3 **announcement** – *Meldung*
4 **to hit the sack** – *ins Bett gehen*
5 **to settle down** – *sich beruhigen*
6 **to snore** – *schnarchen*

TR. 05 The second day begins as the first had ended. And the rain, it rains every day… Meik takes pity on[1] us because of the awful weather and agrees to let us have breakfast in the farmhouse. This revives my spirits[2] so much that, against all expectations[3], I actually manage to saddle[4] my bike afterwards. Even though my bum is screaming, "Don't do it! Don't do it!" I grit my teeth and pedal like I want to win the Tour de France. And I almost do. I keep imagining I'm Jan Ullrich making a final sprint for the yellow jersey[5], but the shiny yellow object in front of me is only Meik's anorak, and it's simply impossible to catch up with the guy. In the end I drop back[6] and wait for Franzi to catch up with me. "But I'll get him in the time trial[7]," I gasp[8].

"Time trial?" Franzi looks across at me, puzzled[9]. She obviously doesn't know much about professional cycling. But who cares! Bastian whizzes past[10] us, and Mona pulls up alongside. She seems to have had a good night's sleep and is in a cheerful mood.

"Turn on the sun!" she says to me.

"Sure, no problem. Where's the switch[11]?"

· · · · · · · · ·

1 **to take pity on sb.** – *Mitleid mit jdm. haben*
2 **to revive spirits** – *seine gute Laune erneuern*
3 **against all expectations** – *entgegen allen Erwartungen*
4 **to saddle** – *aufsatteln*
5 **yellow jersey** – *gelbe Trikot*
6 **to drop back** – *sich zurückfallen lassen*
7 **time trial** – *Zeitfahren*
8 **to gasp** – *keuchen*
9 **puzzled** – *verblüfft*
10 **to whizz past** – *vorbei flitzen*
11 **switch** – *Schalter*

She laughs. "Maybe we should do a sun dance."

"Sun dance?" Franzi is surprised. "I only know rain dances."

"Oh no!" I exclaim. "We've got enough rain as it is!" After a few hours I'm so soaking wet I could wring myself out[1].

"Let's take a break!" calls Raffi, and we are all in favour[2] of this idea. We find a picnic spot in the woods, which even has a roof over it so we can at least butter our rolls in the dry. The scenery[3] is really quite beautiful, and if the weather was a bit better, we could enjoy it a lot more. If the weather was a bit better! In the meantime news arrives on Greetje's mobile from our chaperone. Van Gogh (and his bike) managed to catch a train home early that morning. He'll have to change trains several times, and it will take him at least five hours to get home, where he plans to jump into his car and join us at our next overnight stay. Well, great! Mona sits very close next to Bastian, and the two of them feed each other pieces of bread and sausage. Sweet. I must try that with Meik! I move up close to him, break off a piece of my roll and am just about to pop it into his mouth with a tasty piece of liver sausage[4] when ironically he says,

. . . .
1 **to wring out** - *auswringen*
2 **to be in favour of sth.** - *für etw. sein*
3 **scenery** - *Landschaft*
4 **liver sausage** - *Leberwurst*

"Look at the two of them. They're like a pair of monkeys. Any moment now Mona will start chewing[1] his food for him."

My hand freezes in mid-air[2] on the way to Meik's face. Then I quickly pull it back before I make a fool of myself[3]. I stuff the piece of roll into my mouth and can't help being annoyed by the fact that Meik is so much less romantic than Bastian.

As we ride on, my mood is as chilly[4] as the air temperature. I sigh. What's wrong with me? Even when I do the same as Mona, I keep putting my foot in it[5], whereas everything she touches seems to turn to gold. But at least I'm not the only unlucky one in our team. My ingenious[6] boyfriend Meik leads us onto a particularly lovely cycle path which only has one little hitch[7]: it stops in the middle of nowhere[8]. When Meik suggests turning around and cycling back to take another path, I think I'm going to have a nervous breakdown[9].

• • • • • • • • •

1 **to chew** – *kauen*
2 **in mid-air** – *mitten in der Luft*
3 **to make a fool of oneself** – *sich lächerlich machen*
4 **chilly** – *kühl*
5 **to put one's foot in it** – *ins Fettnäpfchen treten*
6 **ingenious** – *erfinderisch*
7 **hitch** – *Haken*
8 **in the middle of nowhere** – *wo sich Fuchs und Hase gute Nacht sagen*
9 **nervous breakdown** – *Nervenzusammenbruch*

"How many kilometres is that then?" Franzi asks as she hops uncomfortably from one foot to the other. Her bum is obviously sore[1] as well.

Meik ums and ahs. "Yeah, well… to be honest, there's only one other path and… to get there we'd have to… let's just say… well, I'd say…"

"How many?!" Even Bastian is unimpressed[2].

"Ten to fifteen kilometres."

"No! That can't be true!" shrieks[3] Franzi.

"What if we go over the fields to the next road? We don't always have to take the scenic route[4]," suggests Lea. "You can't see anything in the rain anyway."

"Exactly. The quickest way is the best way," I agree with her. So we all soon agree – although Meik strongly advises us against it – and we continue cross-country[5]. The first bit, on a timber path through the woods, is bumpy[6] but just about rideable. But then that comes to an end, and we have to push our bikes through the undergrowth[7]. I think of Livingstone, the rainforest, luggage-bearers[8] sinking[9] into the bog – pure adventure! We have it all, just with bikes instead of luggage-bearers, and it's us who are sinking deeper and deeper into the wet forest floor.

• • • • • • • • •

1 **sore** – *schmerzhaft*
2 **unimpressed** – *wenig begeistert*
3 **to shriek** – *schreien*
4 **scenic route** – *Aussichtsstraße*
5 **cross-country** – *querfeldein*
6 **bumpy** – *uneben*
7 **undergrowth** – *Gestrüpp*
8 **luggage bearer** – *Gepäckträger*
9 **to sink** – *heruntergehen*

"An edible mushroom! Look, a huge edible mushroom!" exclaims Mona all of a sudden[1], really excited. For God's sake, how can anybody notice something like that in this situation? I wouldn't even notice if a big snake hung down from one of the branches and licked my face.

"Leave it," says Bastian to Mona as she's about to pluck[2] it out of the ground. "We can't cook it."

"That's a shame[3]! Then I'll take a photo." Mona takes her camera out of her bag and – click! – the mushroom is in the can[4].

Eventually we come to a forest fence[5].

"Let's look for the gate," suggests Meik. "Most of the time fields have farms nearby, and that means there will be roads, too." That would make me so happy, I think, as I look at my muddy trainers. My feet are already soaking wet, and it wouldn't have made any difference to me if this jungle trip continued with a march through some soggy grassland. For a change I was Atréju on his way to the ancient Morla. The main thing is this trip won't turn into a story to be told for years to come!

But my imagination is soon used up. Pushing loaded bicycles over fields is so tiring that I'm soon sweating[6], not just all over my body, but in my brain as well. I can't even think. I just stagger[7] half dead behind the others, taking it

· · · · · · · · ·

1 **all of a sudden** - *plötzlich*
2 **to pluck** - *pflücken*
3 **that's a shame** - *das ist schade*
4 **in the can** - *im Kasten*
5 **fence** - *Zaun*
6 **to sweat** - *schwitzen*
7 **to stagger** - *taumeln*

step by step. There is no way back… da-dam! We have to pass through a flock[1] of sheep, but what would normally have received cries of delight, is now a smelly nightmare. Damn, they smell like a lorry full of wet jumpers without fabric softener[2]. Hardly Spring fresh! Then come the cows. Black and white ones. Big. Huge. Wild and dangerous!

"For goodness sake, girl! They're cows, not Spanish bulls," says Meik as Lea refuses to go past the animals.

"And how do you know?"

"Look at them! Can't you see what's hanging between their legs? Do they look like bulls to you?" I look as well. No, those udders full of milk don't remind me of bulls at all. They are clearly cows. Dairy cows!

Greetje throws down her bicycle. "I'll milk[3] one of them," she says. "A sip[4] of warm milk right now would do nicely."

"You're mad!"

"Why? Come on, bring your plastic cups over. I milked a fake cow at an agricultural show[5] in Holland once."

"But this one's real," I quickly point out. And it has four legs to walk away on. Which is what it does when Greetje grabs its udders[6]. The cow gives itself a shake, wobbling[7] its udders to and fro[8], and the milk spurts[9] right into Bas-

• • • • • • • • •

1 **flock** – *Herde*
2 **fabric softener** – *Weichspüler*
3 **to milk** – *melken*
4 **sip** – *Schlückchen*
5 **agricultural show** – *Landwirtschaftsaustellung*
6 **udders** – *Euter*
7 **to wobble** – *schwabbeln*
8 **to and fro** – *hin und her*
9 **to spurt** – *spritzen*

tian's face instead of into the cup he's holding out. Then the cow escapes to one side, hits Franzi across the face with its tail and knocks Raffi over [1] with its large backside. He falls back with a cry and lands bum-first in a warm cowpat [2].

"I want to go home!" cries Franzi as she takes in the smelly catastrophe.

I could have had all of this in southern Germany, I think to myself. But in a more hygienic setting of disposable nappies [3]! The cleaning process takes some time, though Franzi eventually manages to talk Raffi into stripping off [4]. There's no way he can continue cycling with his dirty trousers.

So the day's journey goes on, but at some point – though only just – we arrive half dead and completely exhausted at the farm where we can sleep for the night.

TR. 06 "I'm not cycling any further!" The next morning, Franzi decides to go on strike [5]. Maybe I should do the same? But Meik and Bastian take out the maps and show us that it really isn't all that far to the ferry to Wangerooge now. Even if it's still raining, the last leg looks pretty easy-going.

"Where's van Gogh got to?" I dare to ask. Not that I can't get by without a chaperone, but he said he was going to

· · · · · · · · ·

1 **to knock sb. over** – *jdn. umhauen*
2 **cowpat** – *Kuhfladen*
3 **nappies** – *Windeln*
4 **to strip off** – *etw. abstreifen*
5 **to go on strike** – *streiken*

43

join us here.

"The bike rack[1] on his car is broken. He had to order a spare part[2], and it only arrived this morning. He said he'd meet us at the ferry." Meik grins as he tells us about this change of plan[3].

I have to smile to myself too. If it goes on like this, the trip will be over before our chaperone even gets here.

"Our ferry leaves at four o'clock. We shouldn't have any problem making it. And if we leave straight away, it'll be easy," explains Meik, hurrying us along[4]. OK, OK! Take it easy! If only reality always reflected the theory, but, of course, it never does. This time it's my fault. No, I don't fall into a cowpat – at least I'm spared[5] that – but I do get a flat tyre[6] about ten kilometres from the ferry port. This happens about an hour and a half before the ferry sets sail.

"Right, let's get this sorted out then!" says Meik, quite the happy handyman, as he pulls off my basket with Bastian and turns the bike upside down[7]. "Where's your spare inner tube[8]?"

"Er, inner tube? What?"

"Don't tell me you took a trip like this without any spare parts?"

· · · · · · · · ·

1 **bike rack** – *Fahrradträger*
2 **spare part** – *Ersatzteil*
3 **change of plan** – *Planänderung*
4 **to hurry along** – *zur Eile antreiben*
5 **to be spared** – *verschont werden*
6 **flat tyre** – *Reifenpanne*
7 **upside down** – *verkehrt herum*
8 **inner tube** – *Fahrradschlauch*

"Erm, yes, well, to be perfectly honest… I don't usually take trips like this… so I don't normally need anything…" Meik resigns himself to this piece of information and goes over to his basket.

"Alright, I'll use mine then." But he smiles as soon as he sees the miserable look on my face.

"At least it'll stay in the family!" It's so sweet the way he says it. I immediately forgive him for his arrogant[1] tone and make out that only men can repair bicycles. I mean, if it's so important to him, then I don't have to get my hands dirty[2] myself. I'm not half as bothered as him. But I soon gather that things aren't really going to plan by the way Meik and Bastian keep cursing. Franzi starts to get nervous and keeps looking at her watch.

"Come on, boys," she says. "We have to get a move on. Otherwise the ferry will leave without us."

After what seems like an eternity[3] the experts finish up, and we get back on our bikes.

It's now a race against time. "We'll never make it!" I keep thinking as I pedal like a madwoman[4]. This time I would win any time trial, but will that be enough for us to catch the ferry? I don't feel the rain anymore. Besides, sweat is streaming down[5] my bright red face and the gallons of water in and outside my clothes are mixing together. I am

· · · · · · · · ·
1 **arrogant** – *hochmütig*
2 **to get your hands dirty** – *sich die Hände schmutzig machen*
3 **eternity** – *Ewigkeit*
4 **madwoman** – *Verrückte*
5 **to stream down** – *herunterströmen*

hot and my breathing is short. I'm just thinking that I'm going to fall off my bike any second when I see the white buildings of the harbour[1]! Our ferry sounds its foghorn[2]. Oh no, it's going to set sail[3] in front of our very eyes! That would just be so cruel! We sprint over to the dock and would have rushed straight onto the ferry had a sailor not been standing on the gangway[4]. He asks us for our tickets and tells us that, needless to say, our bikes have to be taken on board at a different place. They are as stubborn as German Rail.

We are all looking so completely shattered[5] that thankfully the guy doesn't make any trouble. After briefly looking at his watch, he calls over two colleagues who take our bikes on board[6] before we even know it. We get on just as quickly and drop into the seats in the passenger hall. Dry at last! I shoot up from my seat a few seconds later when Greetje shrieks. She jumps up and throws her arms around her dad's neck. He'd made it to the ferry only a few minutes after us. Well then, everything's perfect!

The youth hostel on Wangerooge is in a tower and it's really great. We girls have a big cosy bedroom just for us and the first thing we do is go to bed. And we sleep like logs[7]!

· · · · · · · · ·

1 **harbour** – *Hafen*
2 **foghorn** – *Nebelhorn*
3 **to set sail** – *lossegeln*
4 **gangway** – *der Laufsteg*
5 **shattered** – *erschöpft*
6 **on board** – *an Bord*
7 **to sleep like a log** – *wie ein Murmeltier schlafen*

The next day it's misty[1], but – what a miracle! – it's dry.
"Come on, Kiki, I'll show you the beach." Meik and I go
past the groynes[2] hand in hand until we come to a really
pretty beach of sand dunes. It's low tide[3], and the water is
leaving behind all sorts of flotsam and jetsam[4], which the
seagulls are swooping down[5] on with shrill cries, in search
of something edible.

"Oh, look!" exclaims Meik all of a sudden. He bends over
and picks something up. When he turns around to me,
he's got a huge smile on his face. "Put your hands out."

I hesitate, because I think he might be winding me up[6]
and is going to drop something horrible and slimy[7] into
my hands. Meik gets impatient[8]. He grabs my hand, opens
it and puts something cold inside. What is it? A stone? It's
far too light for that. Curious, I open my hand and stare
inside. Wow, it's fantastic! A huge, honey-coloured lump
of amber[9].

"It's a present," says Meik. "That's the sun we've been missing until now!" As Meik kisses me, the clouds above us
break and a shower of rain pours down. And that's how it
stays for the rest of the holiday – for many a long, wet kiss.
Although Mona, who catches a nasty cold, and the oth-

· · · · · · · · ·

1 **misty** - *nebelig*
2 **groyne** - *Buhne*
3 **low tide** - *Ebbe*
4 **flotsam and jetsam** - *Strandgut*
5 **to swoop down** - *herabschießen*
6 **to wind up** - *jdn. veräppeln*
7 **slimy** - *glitschig*
8 **impatient** - *ungeduldig*
9 **amber** - *Bernstein*

ers in the group continue to despair at[1] the bad weather, I find the pot of gold[2] at the end of the rainbow[3]. I have my own sun – my amber sun – and, believe me, it warms my heart, that's for sure! We make a hole[4] in it, and I wear it around my neck on a leather string. I win the bad-weather bet but, despite the rain, I had the best holiday a girl could wish for.

TR. 07 Dad takes pity on me. "What a rainy holiday," he says sympathetically[5]. "Listen, I've got a few air miles[6] left. How about three days in Mallorca?" What a question. Hello, sun, here I come! A few hours later I'm lying by the pool. It's just like last year. Same hotel, same swimming pool, same rep. André welcomes me with an "hola, guapa!" Then he throws one of the many bikini beauties[7] into the water, presumably[8] to give them a lesson in underwater kissing. He fools around just like back then, a big friendly bear with a sense of fun, who sings into the mini-disco microphone, "If you're happy on vacation, clap your hands…" He jumps around on the open-air[9] stage, and I watch him from my deckchair[10]. Last year I gave it everything and did the club dance myself. The sun

· · · · · · · · ·

1 **to despair at** – *an etw. verzweifeln*
2 **pot of gold** – *Goldschatz*
3 **rainbow** – *Regenbogen*
4 **hole** – *Loch*
5 **sympathetically** – *mitfühlend*
6 **air miles** – *Bonusmeilen*
7 **bikini beauty** – *Strandschönheit*
8 **presumably** – *vermutlich*
9 **open-air** – *Freiluft-*
10 **deckchair** – *Liegestuhl*

shines. I sigh, flick through[1] my cheeky girls' book and think about Meik, the rainy cycle tour, and the many wet kisses. The amber stone is hanging around my neck. What on earth am I doing here? "Dad," I ask. "When are we flying home?"

```
Love-Question 3
☑ INBOX
from: Meik Mobile


It's no fun without u
at home. Miss u babe!
When r u coming back?
xxx
```

· · · · · · · · ·

1 **to flick through** – *durchblättern*

Bianka Minte-König

Kisses in the Snow

"Marcus, don't!" Kiwi yelps[1] like an injured[2] animal as an avalanche[3] sends him rolling down to the ground. Well, not quite, but the huge snow-ball does push him back a good few metres. After flattening[4] Kiwi, it continues on its way down the hill. Kiwi lies on his back like a wounded goat, throwing his arms and legs around helplessly in the snow. By the time he finally manages[5] to get up, he leaves an angel-like impression of himself in the blanket of white snow. That really doesn't seem right! Kiwi and an angel! "Don't stare like that, Mila!" he moans[6] at me, again not at all angelic. Angel? Disgusting would be more appropriate[7]. Why this guy always has to hang around[8] with us is anyone's guess![9]

"This is all your fault!" says Hannah, still annoyed. "If you weren't with Marcus we wouldn't have to put up with[10] his weird friend."

Unfortunately she's right. But does she think that I like the fact that Marcus always has Kiwi and Knolle in tow[11]? Even on the toboggan run[12].

· · · · · · · · ·

1 **to yelp** – *jaulen*
2 **injured** – *verletzt*
3 **avalanche** – *Lawine*
4 **to flatten** – *niederwalzen*
5 **to manage** – *schaffen*
6 **to moan** – *raunzen*
7 **more appropriate** – *treffender*
8 **to hang around** – *herumhängen*
9 **anyone's guess** – *reine Vermutung*
10 **to put up with** – *ertragen*
11 **in tow** – *im Schlepptau*
12 **toboggan run** – *Rodelbahn*

"Help him," I say to Marcus. "Help him again this time. But next time he comes with us and is so stupid, we will leave him to rot on the slopes[1]."

Marcus smirks.[2] "Nothing would rot at this temperature – not even Kiwi."

"Fine, then he'll just freeze."

"For how long?"

"For the whole of the ski trip. Nobody would notice if he wasn't there. Knolle would just keep on drinking his home brew." Marcus laughs like Santa Claus, with a deep and manly voice. All he needs now are the matching reindeer - he already has a red nose like Rudolph. "And how do we thaw[3] him out again?" I ask, continuing the joke.

Marcus smirks: "Perhaps with a hot kiss?"

I give him a shove[4] and jump on the sledge[5] again.

"Not from me though!" I shout firmly[6]. I wrap my arms around him[7] and we whizz[8] down the hill again on a wild ride. There is powdered snow all around us, kicked up from Hannah and Brian's skis, and Katie and Toby's. I shriek[9] enthusiastically as the cold snowflakes land on my skin. What fun!

· · · · · · · · ·

1 **on the slopes** – *auf der Piste*
2 **to smirk** – *grinsen*
3 **to thaw out** – *auftauen*
4 **to give sb. a shove** – *jdn. schubsen*
5 **sledge** – *Schlitten*
6 **firmly** – *bestimmt*
7 **wrap my arms around him** – *meine Arme um ihn schlingen*
8 **to whizz** – *sausen*
9 **to shriek** – *kreischen*

Our school is on holiday in Switzerland and we are split into two groups, each living with a teacher in a self-catering log cabin[1]. My group is lucky because we have the new biology teacher Mrs Earlyriser[2], while the older pupils have to deal with[3] our P.E. teacher[4], Mr Sprinter. We get back from tobogganing to find a cosy fire crackling[5] in the sitting room of our cabin. Katie, Hannah and I snuggle[6] up together under a blanket, warming our slightly frozen feet and slowly thawing them out. We have mugs of steaming[7] fruit tea beside us and I tell them about the conversation I had with Marcus about Kiwi, who, against all expectations, did reach the bottom of the slopes. Hannah reacts to the mention of a hot kiss with a very mischievous[8] glint[9] in her eye and whispers,

"I already know who could give him the thawing kiss."
This is exciting!

"Who? Tell us now!" demands Katie.
Hannah giggles. "Vanessa! Who else?"
Who else? Nobody dislikes Kiwi as much as Vanessa.
"Rubbish!" I say. "There is no way she would do that." "She would," insists Hannah.

• • • • • • • • •

1 **self-catering log cabin** - *Selbstversorgerhütte*
2 **early riser** - *Frühaufsteher*
3 **to have to deal with** - *herumplagen*
4 **P.E. teacher** - *der Sportlehrer*
5 **to crackle** - *knistern*
6 **to snuggle** - *kuscheln*
7 **steaming** - *dampfend*
8 **mischievous** - *verschmitzt*
9 **glint** - *Glitzern*

"Never!"

"I bet you!"

But I just stare at Hannah in complete bewilderment. [1] Surely she doesn't actually want to bet with me that Vanessa and Kiwi will ever kiss each other of their own free will [2]? And a forced peck on the cheek [3] during spin-the-bottle [4] doesn't really count.

"Not just some time in her life. Here and now. During the ski trip. It is long overdue [5]!" The girl has brain freeze [6]! So, as her good friend I ask her caringly, "Did you forget to wear your hat?"

"Hat? What do you mean?" She looks at me, confused.

"Well, I get the impression [7] that your little grey cells are not working. Perhaps they're frozen ..."

Hannah smirks. "That's what you think! No, no, I am perfectly sane [8]. So where do we stand? Is the bet on?"

"You mean, you really want to bet that Vanessa and Kiwi will get together on this ski trip?" Katie is hardly under the blanket anymore. She is kicking her legs like a sheep being clipped [9] and can't stop giggling. But now she says: "And what are we betting for?"

· · · · · · · · · ·

1 **in complete bewilderment** – *verblüfft*
2 **of their own free will** – *freiwillig*
3 **forced peck on the cheek** – *Zwangsbussi*
4 **spin-the-bottle** – *Flaschendrehen*
5 **overdue** – *überfällig*
6 **brain freeze** – hier: *eingefrorenes Gehirn*
7 **I get the impression** – *ich habe den Eindruck*
8 **sane** – *zurechnungsfähig*
9 **like a sheep being clipped** – *wie ein Schaf bei der Schur*

Yes, what for? A bet without a wager[1] just doesn't work, even if the bet is a stupid one. Hmm, maybe this is a chance to get out of this nonsense.

"So then", I try to put it diplomatically, "Katie is absolutely right, Hannah. If you can think of a good wager then we can talk about it again. Till then, we'll put the whole thing on the backburner[2]." Oh dear! Hannah is not at all pleased with this, but because Brian and Toby come in and obviously do not want to sit under the blanket with us, we leave the topic for now[3]. We make a cosy circle, which Marcus joins. At least he brought another blanket with him, otherwise it would have been a bit tight. As it is though, it's really cosy. The wood crackles[4] in the fireplace and a homely smell[5] of pine trees and fir trees spreads around the room. I lean against Marcus' muscular chest and sigh contently. What do I care[6] if Kiwi and Vanessa kiss or not! "I love you Marcus," I whisper. And while his hand softly strokes my cheek[7], he hums into my ear:
"I like the sound of that, I feel the same way."

· · · · · · · · · ·

1 **wager** – *der Wetteinsatz*
2 **to put on the backburner** – *auf Eis legen*
3 **for now** – *fürs Erste*
4 **to crackle** – *knistern*
5 **homely smell** – *heimeliger Duft*
6 **what do I care** – *was ist mir das schnurzpiepegal*
7 **to stroke a cheek** – *die Wange streicheln*

TR. 02 So, the bet. Having thought about it, us three girls think the bet is pretty stupid, but the idea of Vanessa getting together with Kiwi on the other hand is really cool. And because it's going to be anything but easy we decide that instead of working against each other for a bet, it would be better to use our collective girl power to achieve this higher goal.

"Ha, Vanessa is never going to escape us!" giggles Katie again as we come to this decision[1] at breakfast. Somehow she already seems to be putting herself forward, so I say slightly sarcastically:

"Come on then, Katie, get your spell book out, with your spells and your recipes for love potions and love dishes and then let's get going!" Katie looks at me somewhat[2] cynically. Does she realise that I am winding her up[3]? No, she doesn't. That girl always takes everything I say at face value[4]. By now she should have realised that I have this horribly unsocial habit[5] of constantly pulling my friends' legs[6]. Till they fall off! ;-) In any case she takes her witchcraft really seriously, even though she knows that she could drive me up into the mountains with that nonsense. OK, admittedly[7] from here it's not that far!

· · · · · · · · ·

1 **to come to a decision** - *einen Entschluss fassen*
2 **somewhat** - *etwas*
3 **to wind up** - *veräppeln*
4 **take at face value** - *etwas für bare Münze nehmen*
5 **horribly unsocial habit** - *schrecklich unsoziale Gewohnheit*
6 **to pull someone's leg** - *jdn. auf den Arm nehmen*
7 **admittedly** - *allerdings*

"Hmmm, then I'll have to look at my moon calendar to see which phase of the moon[1] we are in at the moment. If it's a full moon, we can call upon the *moon goddess.*" Katie gives me a questioning look[2]. After our last attempt at witchcraft, which I would rather not talk about, I burst into fits of laughter[3], just upon hearing the words moon goddess.

"Please, Katie, please!" I manage to say as the laughter is already rolling around my vocal chords[4]. "Not this rubbish about the moon goddess again!"

Hannah adds, "Something a bit more low-key[5] might work better...and to organise a full moon ritual in the icy snow – I don't know. I'd rather make something like a love punch..."

"Yeah, I think so too," I agree with Hannah's suggestion. "Love punch sounds good – lots of it for everyone...That's a really cool idea!" And in my head[6] I can already see everyone snuggling up in the cabin. So much love all around – it would be so cool!

"But magic rituals are much more effective," objects Katie with a whisper, because we are already getting curious looks from Vanessa's table. "If I had a few hairs from each of them or a piece of their clothing...It really wouldn't be difficult. I always have a few magic herbs on me..." She

• • • • • • • • •
1 **phase of the moon** – *Mondphase*
2 **questioning look** – *fragender Blick*
3 **to burst into fits of laughter** – *in Lachkrämpfe ausbrechen*
4 **vocal chords** – *Stimmbänder*
5 **low-key** – *unauffällig*
6 **in my head** – *vor meinem inneren Auge*

is going a bit red because she knows what I think about these superstitions[1]. But because I had tried to talk her out of all of this witchcraft stuff so many times before and never really had much success, I am resigned[2] to it. And so as not to make her angry every time she mentions her silly white magic, I decide to put it down to her troubling[3] family background and tolerate it up to a point. I mean, because Katie's mum owns an esoteric shop. In the meantime[4], the hocus pocus can serve as a joke. After all, life is only really great if you don't take it deadly seriously all of the time. Unfortunately our teachers are of a very different opinion. Sigh! Moan! Grumble! But never mind that[5]! "Well fine then, look it up in your moon calendar and let us know. I'll find all of the ingredients you need for this... err...spell"

TR. 03 It's fate[6]: tonight is a full moon. I gave my word[7] and now after a tiring day on the slopes I have to search for Kiwi and Vanessa's personal possessions.[8] But as Katie, Hannah and a few other people, including Vanessa and Kiwi, are busy organising a Raclette

• • • • • • • • •

1 **superstitions** – *Aberglauben*
2 **to be resigned to sth.** – *sich mit etw. abgefunden haben*
3 **troubling** – *belastend*
4 **in the meantime** – *zwischendurch*
5 **but never mind that** – *nun gut*
6 **fate** – *Schicksal*
7 **to give your word** – *sein Wort geben*
8 **personal possessions** – *persönliche Gegenstände*

evening, this is a great opportunity. I creep into their rooms, collect hairs from their pillows and look for a piece of clothing.

Just as I'm rummaging[1] through Kiwi's clothes, I hear a noise at the door. Without looking closely, I stuff[2] the clothes that I have in my hand into my plastic bag and drop to the floor in a panic. I crawl under the

> Love-Question 1
> ☑ INBOX
> from: Hannah mobile
>
> R u OK there? Omg this is so exciting! We'll make them fall in love! Han xxx

nearest bed as quickly as possible. Not a second too soon! Kiwi and Knolle come in and crash onto the bed I am lying under. The springs squeak[3] and the mattress throws up so much dust, that I think the next time I breathe in I will suffocate[4]. It takes all my effort to suppress[5] my coughing. "It's going to be delicious tonight!" says Knolle as I hear him smack his lips together.
"And what drinks are there going to be?" asks Kiwi.
"Home brew maybe?"

· · · · · · · · ·

1 **to rummage** – *wühlen*
2 **to stuff** – *stopfen*
3 **to squeak** – *quietschen*
4 **to suffocate** – *ersticken*
5 **to suppress** – *unterdrücken*

"No, I don't think so. Earlyriser is no Sprinter. She won't let us have any alcohol. I think she said something about tea. The Swiss would drink tea with these kinds of cheese dishes[1]."

Knolle reacts in disgust. "Teeeaaa?! If possible made from herbs and small flowers – collected by Mrs Earlyriser herself! Yuck![2]"

"We could go down into the village and find some more alcohol," suggests Kiwi.

Yes, do that, but do it quickly before I suffocate under here! But they want to stick around[3]. This is bad. For a start I am slowly becoming claustrophobic[4] and secondly I want to finally get back to Katie and Hannah. How do I manage to get the two of them to leave again quickly? I get lucky, as Knolle begins to tell Kiwi a scary story about a ghost that apparently haunts[5] this area.

"There was once a chalet here and it says in the guest book that the chalet builder still haunts this place. One cold winter's night he sent his son down into the village to get Schnapps. While he was down there the boy got caught in a snow storm and froze to death."

· · · · · · · · ·

1 **cheese dishes** – *Käsegerichte*
2 **yuck** – *Igitt*
3 **to stick around** – *dableiben*
4 **to be claustrophobic** – *Platzangst haben*
5 **to haunt** – *spuken*

"Hmmm," says Kiwi thoughtfully, "maybe it would be better to forget about getting the alcohol then. Not that we would freeze down there, of course!"

"Yeah, but it would be interesting to know who is haunting the place."

That gives me an idea! I let out a really deep snarl[1], from the very back of my vocal chords. It sounds just like a door creaking open. It sounds really scary and has exactly the right effect. Both of them jump up high as if they have been bitten by bed bugs[2] and as they stand in front of the bed Kiwi asks frightened and annoyed,

"What.....what was that?"

"N-n-no idea...a door...?"

"But the door is closed."

"Maybe it's a ghostly door from the other side[3]..."

"Oh my God! Do you mean it's the chalet builder?"

Kiwi is suddenly completely pale and is trembling[4] violently, so much so that even the bed is shaking a bit. I have no choice, I have to snarl again and because I'm also very good at imitating cats I add another purr afterwards.

"I don't care what it is ...I, erm, I'm leaving now," declares Knolle and takes off.

And of course Kiwi is right behind him[5]. As they rush out of the room I hear how he asks Knolle:

· · · · · · · · ·

1 **snarl** – *Knurren*
2 **bed bugs** – *Bettwanzen*
3 **from the other side** – *aus dem Jenseits*
4 **to tremble** – *schlottern*
5 **right behind him** – *sofort hinterher*

"And, erm, where are we going to sleep tonight?"
I wait a moment until the coast is clear[1] before I crawl out from under the bed and tiptoe[2] out of the boys' room. I quickly throw the items[3] into our room and then walk out into the sitting room as if nothing had happened.

Everyone is crouching cosily in front of the fire and waiting for the kitchen staff to finish preparing the raclette. I am in high spirits[4] again and as I go back into the group I say: "Hey guys, is this place haunted? I just bumped into[5] a totally frozen, blue-faced young boy who told me that Kiwi and Knolle sent him down into the valley to get some beer. Unfortunately he froze on the journey. I'm supposed to tell you that he's very sorry." Roaring laughter[6]. Only Kiwi and Knolle's grins look somewhat tortured[7]. And later as we sit around the table and Knolle walks past me, he grumbles[8] at me in a very unfriendly way:
"You were winding us up!"
"Really, do you think so?"
"Yes, I think so."
I shrug my shoulders. "Well, enjoy your meal anyway!"

• • • • • • • • •
1 **the coast is clear** – *die Luft is rein*
2 **to tiptoe** – *schleichen*
3 **items** – *Beutestücke*
4 **in high spirits** – hier: *gut drauf*
5 **to bump into** – *begegnen*
6 **roaring laughter** – *schallendes Gelächter*
7 **tortured** – *gequält*
8 **to grumble** – *motzen*

And so it finally arrives, the hour of witches and white magic! Just before midnight, Katie, Hannah and I creep out of our room, wrapped up warm[1], out into the frosty night. It is a starry night and the full moon sits gleaming and splendid[2] over the snow-covered mountains and immerses[3] everything in its shimmering[4] light. We stand next to each other for a moment, breathlessly[5] staring at the enchanted[6] landscape. Were it not for the witchcraft we would never have enjoyed this kind of night-time experience. Now we are very glad that we did. Even if the magic doesn't work out, we will still have the memory of the Alps at night under the light of the full moon.

"It is wonderful," says Katie, finally breaking the silence. And Hannah, practical as always, adds: "Yes, but if we don't want to freeze out here, we should make a start." And as she speaks, a thick, white cloud of breath emerges from her mouth. It really is horribly cold, much, much colder than during the day and so we quickly begin our witchcraft. Behind the cabin there is a slight dip, which seems to us to be very well suited to our ritual, because we are hidden from view[7] there. Katie digs out her cauldron[8]

· · · · · · · · ·

1 **wrapped up warm** – *dick eingemummelt*
2 **splendid** – *prächtig*
3 **to immerse** – *tauchen*
4 **shimmering** – *flirrend*
5 **breathlessly** – *atemlos*
6 **enchanted** – *verzaubert*
7 **hidden from view** – *vor Blicken geschützt*
8 **cauldron** – *Kessel*

and fire fuel[1] and lights a small fire under the cauldron.

"So," she says, as she gets the aromatic[2] dried herbs out of her bag and throws them into the cauldron. "Where are the personal possessions of our future lovebirds[3]?" Hearing the word "lovebirds" and then thinking of Kiwi and Vanessa tickles my funny bone[4] and I have to laugh before Katie calls the moon goddess. She throws me an angry look in response.

"Mila, if you are going to sabotage[5] the magic with your silliness again then there is no point in starting this."

"No, no," I say sheepishly.[6] "I'm sorry, I won't do it again." Nevertheless, my giggles rage[7] inside me. So as not to get another unfriendly look from Katie, I quickly get out my shopping bag with the items I collected from Vanessa and Kiwi and hand it to Katie. She throws the hairs into the cauldron straight away, along with the strand of wool from Vanessa's scarf. But then she stops in the middle of what she's doing and looks at me annoyed.

"What is THAT?" she asks, tentatively[8] holding up a flimsy[9] bit of white fabric.

· · · · · · · · ·

1 **fire fuel** – *Brennpaste*
2 **aromatic** – *wohlriechend*
3 **lovebirds** – *Turteltauben*
4 **to tickle my funny bone** – *mein Zwerchfell kitzeln*
5 **to sabotage** – *sabotieren*
6 **sheepishly** – *kleinlaut*
7 **to rage** – *toben*
8 **tentatively** – *zögernd*
9 **flimsy** – *labbrig*

"Erm," I stammer[1], and again almost choke on my swallowed laughter[2] "Kiwi's underpants"...? "It was only thing I could grab hold of quickly as he came into the room with Knolle."

Hannah cannot control herself any longer and I lose it as well. The giggling floods out of us and is uncontrollable.

"Er, do you not think it's suitable Katie?"

"Well," she says still sounding a bit alienated[3]. "If you assume that love happens for Kiwi in his pants rather than in his heart...thinking that way...it's very suitable."

So not a mistake, but a stroke of luck.[4]

"But I can hardly put his whole underpants into this small cauldron..." Katie scowls[5] at the intimate piece of clothing.

"Then we'll pull off a thread," suggests Hannah practically. However this proves to be somewhat harder than I thought, as it's tough fabric. I am for the quickest option.

"Then let's cut a small piece out of them."

"Hmm, that would be material damage[6]."

"My goodness, Hannah! Have you learnt the rule book off by heart[7]?"

"No, but maybe he only has the one pair to change into..." As that could well be the case with Kiwi, we forget the idea of cutting a bit out. I take off my gloves and fish out[8]

· · · · · · · · ·

1 **to stammer** – *drucksen*
2 **swallowed laughter** – *unterdrücktes Lachen*
3 **alienated** – *befremdet*
4 **a stroke of luck** – *Glücksgriff*
5 **to scowl** – *missmutig starren*
6 **material damage** – *Sachschaden*
7 **to learn off by heart** – *auswendig lernen*
8 **to fish out** – *pfriemeln*

a piece of cotton from the waistband[1]. That way the pants won't fall apart straight away! I throw the cotton into the witches' cauldron with icy cold fingers, Katie pours a clear liquid[2] over it and sets it alight. A small, blue darting flame[3] flickers up[4].

"What was that?" I ask, interested. Maybe I could impress Marcus with the same rubbish. "What did you flambé it with?"

"What did I use? Schnapps, of course, just like in the finest gourmet restaurants."

My goodness! Katie hustles[5] us all together and demands that we form a circle around the cauldron, hold hands and – yes, I know this is where it gets really silly – call upon the moon goddess. I can't do it, I really can't do it – that's the thought that keeps flashing through my mind[6]. I was unable to do it when we were doing it for Katie to find love and she is one of my best friends. I certainly can't do something like this for Vanessa and Kiwi! Hannah winks[7] at me and hisses softly: "It's just a joke. Just do it!" And so once I put my rational self[8] to one side I grab hold of my friends' hands and step into the magic circle. Smirks!

· · · · · · · · · ·
1 **waistband** – *Hosenbund*
2 **liquid** – *Flüssigkeit*
3 **darting flame** – *Stichflamme*
4 **to flicker up** – *aufzüngeln*
5 **to hustle** – *scheuchen*
6 **to flash through my mind** – *mir durch den Kopf schießen*
7 **to wink at** – *zuzwinkern*
8 **rational self** – *Vernunft-Ich*

Katie raises her eyes to the moon and begins to mumble[1] the magic words very secretively. Finally she says clearly and precisely: "Oh, moon goddess, cement the bond[2] between Kiwi and Vanessa and bless[3] this bond." She lets me go.

"Was that it?" I ask, quite disappointed. "Don't we also have to..."

Katie shakes her head, throwing snow at the cauldron and immediately putting out[4] the flame, explaining: "No, it's not necessary. It just takes a little bit of magic."

Hmm, bringing Vanessa and Kiwi together is just a little bit of magic? If she's not deluding[5] herself! As we slip back into the house and go past Knolle and Kiwi's room, I pull his pants out of the bag and hang them on the door handle. Ta da, Santa's been!

TR. 04 Of course the next morning he wants to know who did this and isn't satisfied with the Santa Claus explanation. But because we keep an icy silence, unfortunately he has no chance of getting to the bottom of[6] this secret act.

· · · · · · · · ·

1 **to mumble** - *murmeln*
2 **to cement the bond** - *das Band knüpfen*
3 **to bless** - *segnen*
4 **to put out** - *löschen*
5 **to delude oneself** - *sich täuschen*
6 **to get to the bottom of sth.** - *etw. aufklären*

"It really seems to be haunted here," I say to stress them both out a bit more. "The chalet builder probably slept in your room before, or else why would the ghost only show himself to you."

"Can we have a different room?" I hear Kiwi ask Mrs Earlyriser shortly afterwards[1].

She just shrugs her shoulders. "And where would you go? You know yourself that we are taking up[2] all the rooms and beds. You can only have another room if you can find someone to swap with you." But who would volunteer[3] to sleep in a haunted room?

The really cool thing about this year's ski trip is that it takes place during Fasching. This means that being on the slopes on Rosenmontag is definitely going to be lots of fun. As early as Saturday, they were beginning to build an ice bar at the foot of the small beginners' slope behind the cabin. Mr Sprinter's group from the neighbouring cabin[4] is also getting involved and it's going to be really impressive[5]. We pile up snow in heaps and create a proper bar, a space for the barbecue[6] and even benches and bar stools[7]. In the afternoon I snuggle up with Hannah and Katie, exhausted but warm underneath the blanket in the sitting room, whispering about Kiwi and Vanessa.

. . . .

1 **shortly afterwards** - *kurz danach*
2 **to take up** - *belegen*
3 **to volunteer for** - *sich freiwillig melden*
4 **the neighbouring cabin** - *die Nachbarhütte*
5 **impressive** - *beeindruckend*
6 **barbecue** - *Grill*
7 **bar stools** - *Barhocker*

"Katie, are you sure the magic is going to work? Somehow I'm not seeing any progress."

Hannah agrees, as it is quite obvious that the opposite is happening. After the business with Kiwi's pants, Vanessa made a few mean comments about unfashionable men's underwear and while the ice bar was being built, Kiwi got his own back by burying[1] her hand in the snow, for which Vanessa turned the main water pipe off in the shower. Kiwi had already lathered himself up[2] and waited for someone to turn it on again for about ten minutes. Finally he lost his patience[3] and screamed for help. As Katie, the Mother Teresa figure as ever, rushed over and wanted to know what was wrong, he threw open the shower door butt naked[4] and bellowed[5] at her:

"Can't someone get the stupid water running again!"

Although the foam[6] covered him like a fur coat, Katie still had to make sure she didn't look at him too closely. She grabbed the door out of his hand and slammed[7] it shut again. This led to an outburst of cursing[8] as it seemed she had banged it against his nose.

"Well," Katie continues the story with a smirk, "then I saw Vanessa giggling in the corner with Carmen. They were standing directly in front of the water connection and the

· · · · · · · · ·

1 **to bury** – *einmauern*
2 **lathered up** – *eingeschäumt*
3 **to lose patience** – *Geduld verlieren*
4 **butt naked** – *splitternackt*
5 **to bellow** – *brüllen*
6 **foam** – *Schaum*
7 **to slam** – *zuschlagen*
8 **a tirade of curses** – *ein Schwall von Flüchen*

70

hot water tank, so of course I thought that they had some-
thing to do with it"
"And you turned the water on again?"
She cracks up with laughter[1]. "Yes, but only the cold tap..."
We can easily picture how Kiwi would have run away and
she only has to mention his squeals[2] for Hannah and I to
burst out laughing as well.
"Why is everyone always so mean to Kiwi in particular?"
Katie suddenly asks.
Hmm, I'm not really sure. "Maybe because he always
seems so stupid?"
"Yeah, he's not the brightest[3]," agrees Hannah.
"Perhaps he is also a bit challenged[4]...in terms of his devel-
opment," says Katie trying to defend him. "He is actually
quite funny but in terms of his thoughts he never really
seems to be quite there most of the time..."
"...he is thinking about some dream woman with big boo-
bs and a fat bum!" I say mercilessly.[5] Sympathy[6] for Kiwi
is the last thing I need to feel. First of all he needs to learn
how to behave! And because all three of us think that he
has already gone through puberty, we all think it's really
important to get him together with Vanessa. I mean, they
should both have the emotional maturity that comes with
going through puberty.

· · · · · · · · · ·

1 **to crack up with laughter** – *herzhaft lachen*
2 **squeals** – *Schreie*
3 **the brightest** – *der Hellste*
4 **challenged** – *behindert*
5 **mercilessly** – *gnadenlos*
6 **sympathy** – *Mitleid*

71

"Are you sure that *we* already have this, er, emotional maturity?", asks Hannah, looking very doubtful[1].

Katie and I look at each other. We are probably both thinking about the night of the full moon, which really doesn't say much in our favour and so once again we break into silly giggling and ignoring reality we say almost in unison[2], "But of course!"

Marcus, Toby and Brian come in and of course they want to know what's going on. But we remain tight-lipped[3].

"Girl talk, it's none of your business."

"That's a shame," says Marcus, "We wanted to snuggle up with you and play music."

Brian has his guitar with him and looks somewhat disappointed at Hannah's rebuff[4].

"Then go and sit on the bench over there. We just need to discuss something quickly and then we'll sing with you," I give in.

As they play the first guitar chord, we go back to discussing our plan of action.

· · · · · · · · ·
1 **doubtful** – *zweifelhaft*
2 **in unison** – *einstimmig*
3 **tight-lipped** – *verschlossen*
4 **rebuff** – *Abfuhr*

"To get Kiwi and Vanessa together we need something much more powerful than moon magic," I begin. "What about a love dish[1]? Haven't you got lots of experience of making those, Katie?" says Hannah. Katie

```
Love-Question 2
☑ INBOX
from: Marcus

Missing u. Playing
this song 4 u. When
will u come over?
Hurry up with the
girl talk! Mxx
```

looks thoughtful for a moment, which I can understand because as far as I remember it didn't really go 100 per cent to plan[2] last time. But if the right guy had eaten the meal...then who knows what might have happened?

"But," I confirm, "the effect was not bad. Your fat cousin got quite romantic after that."

Katie laughs. "Yes, it was really intense...The only thing is it is a very precise, intricate[3] recipe. There's no way I'll be able to put it together here." And she quickly goes through a list of the ingredients in her head. "Jelly, candles, a few rose petals[4]..." She looks at us confused. "Where am I supposed to find roses in the winter wilderness?[5]"

Alas, where shall I take, when
Winter comes, the flowers, and where
The sunshine ...[6]

· · · · · · · · ·

1 **love dish** - *Liebesspeise*
2 **it didn't go to plan** - *es hat nicht geklappt*
3 **intricate** - *aufwendig*
4 **petals** - *Blütenblätter*
5 **winter wilderness** - *Wintereinsamkeit*
6 **aus ,Hälfte des Lebens' von Friedrich Hölderlin** - *Weh mir, wo nehm' ich, wenn es Winter ist, die Blumen her und wo den Sonnenschein ...*

The first few lines of a poem by Hölderlin come into my mind and then I get an idea. "Would dried petals work?" I ask. "I have a pomander[1] with rose petals and lavender in. I put it in-between my clothes."

"That could work," Katie is prepared to make compromises. "But what about the other ingredients?"

"Down in the village shop. We could nip down there[2]."

"On our own? Just the three of us?" my friends don't like the idea.

And so I jump up from the sofa and go over to the boys. "Hey guys, do you want to spend the rest of the day crouching[3] behind the stove? It's a bit too early to be doing that! Who wants to come with us to the village?" After the tiring morning we have had, they aren't very enthusiastic either. But as we get ready to go down to the valley nonetheless, without the boys if necessary, they gather themselves up[4] and we meet in the ski room a little bit later.

It's still bright enough to ski down and we can get the chair-lift[5] back. By the time we are standing in front of the cabin, with our boards[6] on, we are all feeling energetic again and with a loud cry we head into the evening sun, onto the slopes and down into the village. There we

· · · · · · · · ·

1 **pomander** - *Duftbeutel*
2 **nip down there** - *runterfahren*
3 **to crouch** - *hocken*
4 **to gather yourself up** - *sich aufraffen*
5 **chair lift** – *Sessellift*
6 **boards** - *Bretter*

go into a tea shop and all drink Jagertee, which Marcus treats us to. The waitress puts even less alcohol in the tea than usual but we stroll[1] around the village in a very high spirits[2] nonetheless. We are so lively[3] that some adults try to avoid us, shaking their heads disapprovingly[4] at the youth of today. There's some done-up bimbo[5] – Gucci sunglasses, fur boots and a fur cap – with a badly tanned wannabe celebrity on her arm who obviously thinks that her visitor's tax[6] includes ownership of all of the pathways in the village. She doesn't even think of letting us pass and instead remains right in the middle of the path, breaking up our chain. Well Marcus and Brian break up their bimbo-celeb-two-person chain as payback[7] and carry her along with them, laughing. The guy looks back at us in amazement and right away she begins to clamour[8] for him, not finding it in the slightest bit funny.

"Let her go," advises Katie scared, as she doesn't want any trouble.

And as if following orders Marcus and Brian let her go at exactly the same time. The bimbo falls into a pile of snow on the roadside, which comes up to her tummy, and keeps on screeching[9] and paddling with her arms as if you could

. . . .
1 **to stroll** – *schlendern*
2 **in very high spirits** – *in sehr aufgeräumter Stimmung*
3 **lively** – *lebhaft*
4 **disapprovingly** – *missbilligend*
5 **bimbo** – *Tussi*
6 **visitor's tax** – *Kurtaxe*
7 **as payback** – *zum Ausgleich*
8 **to clamour** – *zetern*
9 **to screech** – *kreischen*

just swim out of a pile of snow. As if! We have already disappeared round the next corner by the time her guy reaches her and she manages to get herself up with the help of his white hands. I don't know who he reminds me of, but nevertheless I'm sure that I saw him photographed with another woman in a gossip mag[1] only recently. Which of them he was cheating on[2] with whom isn't clear but he definitely deserves[3] to be punished for that. Well, keep digging yourself out, I think without sympathy. We get away from the boys and head to the village shop where we manage to get everything that we need for our love dish including, of course, really nice red jelly. We buy more packets than we need as Hannah says that if we're cooking anyway we can make a few more bowls and take them down to the ice bar to feed to people on Rosenmontag.

"Great," I agree. "And we can use that as an opportunity to secretly[4] give Kiwi and Vanessa their love dish."

We meet the boys at the chair lifts. Marcus and I squeeze in[5] next to each other on a two-person lift, he takes me in his arms and I lean against him. The chair sways through the cold darkness up the mountain and our kisses keep us warm. Life is just great again!

· · · · · · · · ·

1 **gossip mag** – *Klatschblatt*
2 **to cheat on sb.** – *jdn. betrügen*
3 **to deserve** – *verdienen*
4 **secretly** – *unauffällig*
5 **to squeeze in** – *quetschen*

TR. 05 They finish the ice bar on Sunday and Sprinter's group mark out a fun slalom, finishing right by the bar. Perfect to get your energy back at the end! It's going to be so much fun! While most people are helping, we are busy in the kitchen preparing the love dish and love punch. For both recipes it's vital[1] to have roses and to utter[2] the magic words by candlelight[3]. Katie and Hannah carry out the ritual while I decide to stand on guard[4] at the door so that nobody can interrupt[5] the magic. To be honest[6] I am really pleased to have this job as I'm not convinced that my negative karma didn't ruin the magic last time. So that I don't have to join in with this rubbish this time, I am in charge of[7] constantly getting rid of[8] people who really want to come in the kitchen.

"You can't come in," I say to Vanessa. "You really can't. It's a surprise for Rosenmontag."

And that's true. Roses for Rosenmontag. Flowers of love for her and Kiwi. As I think about it, I really have to force myself to keep a straight face[9]... In the mean time, Hannah and Katie finish their ritual and put the rose petals into a bowl, over which they pour the jelly. The rest of the red liquid will fill two other bowls without any magic

· · · · · · · · ·

1 **vital** – *unverzichtbar*
2 **to utter** – *sprechen*
3 **by candlelight** – *bei Kerzenlicht*
4 **to stand on guard** – *Schmiere stehen*
5 **to interrupt** – *unterbrechen*
6 **to be honest** – *ehrlich gesagt*
7 **to be in charge of** – *für etw. verantwortlich sein*
8 **to get rid of** – *abwimmeln*
9 **to keep a straight face** – *ernst zu bleiben*

ingredients. I don't need to stand on guard any longer and after the dessert cools we cover it in aluminium foil and put it in the big fridge to set[1].

"Great," I say, satisfied. "Then let's see if Katie's witchcraft really works."

She frowns at me[2]. "So you still believe in the power of white magic?"

I smirk. "If you're asking me honestly Katie," I say diplomatically, "I believe in the magic of love and that should be enough."

In the evening we sit in the sitting room in small groups, feasting on[3] cheese fondue. Five to six people share one pot of fondue and it's wonderfully cosy because we and the boys have the table right next to the crackling tile stove[4]. Later on we play some more music and when we all finally decide to go back to our rooms I am so tired that I immediately fall into a deep sleep. That's why it takes a while for me to realise that somebody is shaking my shoulder. I am so sleepy that I hesitate[5] to open my eyes. It's Katie, who looks like a ghost in her white flannel nightgown.[6]

· · · · · · · · · ·
1 **to set** – *fest werden*
2 **to frown** – *stirnrunzelnd ansehen*
3 **to feast on** – *schlemmen*
4 **crackling tile stove** – *der Kachelofen*
5 **to hesitate** – *zögern*
6 **flannel night gown** – *Flanellnachthemd*

"Wh-wh-what's wrong then?" I ask stroppy[1] and confused.

"There's someone in the kitchen," she whispers.

"So what?" I murmur and turn over to the other side. "As long as the cabin isn't burning down."

"But he...he's doing something in the fridge..."

Even if he is, what do I care? Ah, hang on a minute! I shoot up[2]. "Are you saying that somebody is getting into the fridge?"

"Exactly."

"You don't think that whoever it is is doing something to our love dish?"

"Well, that's what I'm worried about."

I sit up and see that Hannah is standing right behind Katie. She already has her dressing gown[3] on. Obviously she is determined to get to the bottom of[4] what's going on right away. Well then I have to go too! I jump into my slipper socks[5] and throw my dressing gown on too.

"How did you find this out in the first place[6]?" I ask Katie, because after all the kitchen is quite a way away from our room.

"I had to go to the toilet and when I went past the stairs I saw a light coming from the kitchen..."

• • • • • • • • •

1 **stroppy** – *unwirsch*
2 **shoot up** – *hochschießen*
3 **dressing gown** – *Bademantel*
4 **get to the bottom of sth.** – *etw. auf den Grund gehen*
5 **slipper socks** – *Hüttenschuhe*
6 **in the first place** – *überhaupt erst*

79

"OK," I say, keen to find out more. "Then we need to see who it is that we need to stop."

We creep up to the staircase. Katie was right, light is still spilling[1] out of the kitchen into the hallway. We tiptoe[2] down the staircase, sneak along and lurk[3] outside the kitchen. Oops! We almost bump heads. Look at that! Mrs Earlyriser and Sprinter are sitting cosily at the kitchen table eating from one of our big bowls of jelly! They seem to be having a great time as every now and again we hear a shy giggle from her or a muffled[4] laugh from him. We slowly move back a bit.

"That's awful!" moans Katie, looking pale. "Can anyone see which bowl it is?"

I shake my head. How could anyone see from this distance? The rose petals are at the very bottom of the bowl. And I don't really understand all the fuss, but *I* also do not believe in the power of the love dish.

It is a different story for Katie. "This can't be happening," she says visibly shaken[5]. "Poor Mrs Earlyriser...Just imagine if Sprinter falls head over heels in love[6] with her – him of all people!"

· · · · · · · · · ·
1 **to spill out** – *fallen*
2 **to tiptoe** – *auf Zehenspitzen schleichen*
3 **to lurk** – *lauern*
4 **muffled** – *dumpf*
5 **visibly shaken** – *sichtlich erschüttert*
6 **to fall head over heels in love with** – *sich in jdn. verknallen*

At this point I have to abandon[1] my sense of reason, but Hannah gets in before me.

"Katie, calm down[2]. The whole thing was a bit of fun, a joke, nothing's going to happen."

But this doesn't calm Katie down, instead it makes her angry. "You mean, neither of you believed in it the whole time we were doing it? Why would you even let me do the whole magic thing at all then? That is so two-faced[3] of you! And you call yourself my friends?!" She spits out[4] her words at us so loudly that they can't help but hear it in the kitchen.

Suddenly Mrs Earlyriser stands in the brightly lit doorway and asks into the darkness: "Is someone there? Hello?"

And because I'm feeling a bit naughty again I make my famous, scary door creaking noise and add a small "boo" to go with it.

"Children's heads," she says laughing. "Off you go to bed! If I have to ask you again you will be banned from the slopes tomorrow."

Well we don't want to risk that on Rosenmontag. She gave us a chance to retreat[5], so with that we creep back to our room as quickly as possible.

"And what are we going to do about the love dish?" Katie asks.

· · · · · · · · ·

1 **abandon** – *aufgeben*
2 **to calm down** – *sich beruhigen*
3 **two-faced** – *falsch, heuchlerisch*
4 **to spit out** – *fauchen*
5 **a chance to retreat** – *eine goldene Rückzugsbrücke*

"If they ate it they only have themselves to blame," I explain dryly [1]. "Maybe they were only tucking into [2] the normal jelly. We will find out in the morning."

TR. 06 Of course it was the love dish they were eating. When we look in the morning there is a lot missing from the bowl with the rose petals at the bottom. But because there is still enough there to give to Vanessa and Kiwi we decide to leave it for now and wait and see what happens. At first, nothing. So we prepare the love punch. We take Sprinter' s home brew and pour it over the enchanted [3] rose petals. Ready. Love potion express, so to speak. Special circumstances call for special magic. Even ancient rituals need to be updated [4]. Fast food, fast drink! The party gets going in the late afternoon. The sun is shining bright and warm and we are all dressed up. Most people are wearing pyjamas or nightshirts, but a few, who had realised at home that we would be here during Fasching, are wearing false noses [5], hula skirts [6], colourful shirts or garlands. We are wearing our ski suits underneath though - we don't want to end up as costumed icicles. Of course Kiwi and Knolle look the best again, as they'd ransacked [7] their great grandmothers' linen cupboards [8] and

· · · · · · · · ·

1 **dryly** - *trocken*
2 **to tuck into** - *verputzen*
3 **enchanted** - *verzaubert*
4 **to update** - *modernisieren*
5 **false nose** - *Pappnase*
6 **hula skirts** - *Baströckchen*
7 **ransacked** - *geplündert*
8 **linen cupboard** - *Wäscheschrank*

are wearing their corsages and huge bras with fun feathered hats[1]. The prize for the best costume will definitely go to one of them. This really annoys Vanessa, because she had obviously spent time at home planning how to stand out[2] on the fun slalom. She has a proper Fasching costume and to our horror[3] she looks like a pink ski bunny with pink rabbit ears, a little stumpy tail and a snug[4], plush pink body suit. God, how weird! Marcus and Brian burst out laughing, but Kiwi whistles at her like an idiot. And all of this before he even eats a spoonful of our love dish or takes a swig[5] of our love punch! The event begins with the fun slalom. Mrs Earlyriser leads the whole group up to the start and Sprinter records the time at the bottom with two people from his cabin. We get down to the bottom with our boys fairly well, but some of the others get tangled up[6] in their strange costumes and arrive at the finish line[7] on all fours. Knolle lands on a slalom pole, which of course gives way[8] under his weight and rolls down to the ground with him, taking lots more poles with it along the way. Well, great! This means that Sprinter and a few other people have to straighten up[9] the course again before we can continue.

• • • • • • • •

1 **feathered hat** – *Federhut*
2 **to stand out** – *besonders glänzen*
3 **to our horror** – *zu unserem Entsetzen*
4 **snug** – *eng*
5 **swig** – *Schluck*
6 **to get tangled up** – *sich verheddern*
7 **the finish line** – *Ziellinie*
8 **to give way** – *nachgeben*
9 **to straighten up again** – *wieder richten*

As we have already done our run, we begin to warm up the love punch, while Marcus, Brian and Toby stoke up[1] the barbecue for the sausages with Knolle. As the slalom is put back together, Kiwi takes his run. He is not an exceptionally gifted[2] skier, so he has no choice but to perform a funny run, sometimes skiing on one leg, sometimes sliding on his bum and pulling dangerous stunts[3]. By the end everyone is just pleased that he gets to the finish line with only a few tumbles. Of course the prize for the worst run will go to him.

Vanessa, who goes directly after him obviously sets no store[4] by such honours as she swings her bunny tail, highly focussed and weaving[5] through the poles at breakneck speed[6], making us all hold our breath. She looks so rapid and dangerous. She seems to have made a good time as well, as Sprinter says to her approvingly,

"Hey Vanessa, maybe you should do sport in a rabbit costume more often."

We grin at each other. Typical Sprinter – if he gives someone a compliment[7] he always has to insult them at the same time! Vanessa also picks up on this as she crouches down in front of the bar, frustrated. But it is easy to foist[8] the love drink upon her with the comment:

· · · · · · · ·⁚

1 **to stoke up** – *anheizen*
2 **gifted** – *begnadet*
3 **dangerous stunts** – *halsbrecherische Verrenkungen*
4 **to set no store by sth.** – *keinen Wert auf etw. legen*
5 **to weave** – *sich durchschlängeln*
6 **at breakneck speed** – *mit einem Affentempo*
7 **to give a compliment** – *loben*
8 **to foist** – *unterschieben*

"Come on, have a drink, Sprinter's got a screw loose[1]."
Luckily for us, Kiwi comes to sit down at that same moment and guzzles[2] down his dose of the magic drink.
Great! I am excited to see if it will have the effect Katie predicted – and above all when will it kick in? Finally everyone has had their run on the slalom. Mrs Earlyriser is the last to come down and collects the slalom poles on her way. Sprinter chivalrously[3] runs up to her to help her and take on some of the load. They both keep giggling happily in the process, making us really question whether this could be the first sign of the unwanted effects from their night-time love snack. The barbecue is alight, the sausages smell delicious and taste great and we are drinking Sprinter's home brew. Of course there is also a non-alcoholic version – Mrs Earlyriser had insisted – and there's lots of coke and juice in the ice bar. This means that nobody has to drink Sprinter's swill[4], but as people always like doing what they're not supposed to do we are all keen on it[5]. The punch supply is gone in no time[6] and before we know it, some people have started on our love brew. Oh man! And it's a similar story with the love dish. We have hardly given Kiwi and Vanessa a helping each, before the whole world descends[7] on the bowls of jelly and they are empty in an instant. Now it's time for absolute relaxation, Marcus and

· · · · · · · · ·

1 **to have a screw loose** - *ein Rad abhaben*
2 **to guzzle** - *schlürfen*
3 **chivalrously** - *ganz Kavalier*
4 **swill** - *Gesöff*
5 **to be keen on** – *scharf darauf sein*
6 **in no time** - *in null Komma nichts*
7 **to descend on** – *sich stürzen*

Brian set up a music system and the ice bar turns into a disco with everyone dancing happily. Is it something to do with our magic jelly and punch, that suddenly an amazing amount of couples are in each other's arms?

As it slowly gets dark, the boys light torches[1] that they have lined up in a semi-circle in the snow. It's now time for the prizes to be given out. Suddenly Vanessa and Kiwi are standing together at the front of the stage, which is made out of a few boxes. Vanessa is the quickest woman through the slalom and Kiwi, as we expected, is the funniest skier who managed to make the finish line with his skis on. Vanessa is clearly proud to receive the medal and Kiwi is overwhelmed with joy[2]. He is so excited by this award – probably the first of his life – that he suddenly takes Vanessa into his arms and kisses her. Completely taken aback[3] by his spontaneity, she kisses him back. My goodness! But the stage made out of boxes is not built for this sort of action and collapses. Our cute bunny and the weird guy in grandma's corsage crash down into the snow, clinging to[4] each other tightly. All three of us are sure that it is only our love dish and love drink that is stopping Vanessa ripping him into little pieces in front of everybody and handing them out to bystanders as a small snack. She

• • • • • • • • •
1 **torch** – *Fackel*
2 **overwhelmed with joy** – *vor Freude überwältigt*
3 **taken aback** – *überrumpelt*
4 **to cling to** – *aneinanderklammern*

gathers[1] herself up and has a majestic[2] smile on her face as she gets her act together again. It's a bit crooked[3], but it's a smile nonetheless. And it gets better: she even reaches out her hand to Kiwi, who is still laying bewildered[4] in the broken pile of boxes and pulls him up! His head is glowing bright red like a fire alarm and his face shows his gratitude for this gesture. We burst into fits of giggles and high five[5] each other as Hannah says with a touch of irony: "So, we did it. I bet this is the start of a beautiful friendship!"

At the very same moment, a firework goes off and I melt into Marcus' arms[6]. As he kisses me tenderly with the rockets shooting up above and thousands of colourful stars scattering across the sky, I am sure that his love definitely has nothing to do with the love dish, as neither he nor I have had any to eat. How reassuring[7] and how wonderful!

"Look," Marcus suddenly says and nods in the direction of[8] the ice bar.

No, I can't take anymore! Standing there are Mrs Earlyriser and our P.E. teacher Sprinter and what are they doing? - Cuddling!

· · · · · · · · · ·

1 **to gather oneself up** - *sich zusammennehmen*
2 **majestic** - *erhaben*
3 **crooked** - *schief*
4 **bewildered** - *verdutzt*
5 **to high five** - *jdn. abklatschen*
6 **to melt into his arms** - *in seinen Armen dahinschmelzen*
7 **reassuring** - *beruhigend*
8 **in the direction of** - *in Richtung ...*

SMS-GLOSSAR

camera phone
Foto-Handy

inbox
Eingang

mobile (phone)
Handy

pay as you go
Prepaid

photo message
MMS

predictive text
Texterkennung

text sb.
jdn. ansimsen

text message
SMS

4 — for
für

2 — to; too
zu, auf; auch

2gether — together
zusammen

l8 — late
spät

w8 — wait
warten

b — be
sein

c — see
sehen

r — are
bist, seid

u — you
du, ihr

ur — your; you're
dein, euer; du bist,
ihr seid

hun — honey
Schatz

gonna — going to
werden

alrite — alright/OK
OK, in Ordnung

kinda — kind of
irgendwie

wanna — want to
möchten

lol - laughing out
loud
laut lachend

cul8r - see you later
bis später

b/f - boyfriend
Freund

bday - birthday
Geburtstag

x - kiss
Kuss

NÜTZLICHE AUSDRÜCKE ZUM THEMA LIEBE

ask sb. out	*jdn. zu einem Date einladen*
be crazy / mad about sb.	*für jdn. schwärmen*
be heartbroken	*todunglücklich sein*
be lovesick	*Liebeskummer haben*
chat sb. up	*jdn. anmachen*
chat-up line	*Anmachspruch*
cheat on sb.	*jdn. betrügen*
couple	*Pärchen*
dump sb.	*mit jdm. Schluss machen*
fall in love with sb.	*sich in jdn. verlieben*
have butterflies in one's stomach	*Schmetterlinge im Bauch haben*
hug	*sich umarmen*
in a relationship	*vergeben*
in love	*verliebt*
kiss	*küssen*
loveletter	*Liebesbrief*
single	*Single; solo*
secret note	*Geheimbotschaft*
shy	*schüchtern*
snog	*knutschen*

WORTLISTE

a chance to retreat	*eine goldene Rückzugsbrücke*
a stroke of luck	*Glücksgriff*
a.k.a	*auch bekannt als*
abandon	*aufgeben*
accompany	*begleiten*
ache	*schmerzen*
admittedly	*allerdings*
adventure cycle tour	*Erlebnis-Radtour*
affectionately	*liebevoll*
against all expectations	*entgegen allen Erwartungen*
agenda	*Programm*
agricultural show	*Landwirtschaftsaustellung*
air miles	*Bonusmeilen*
aisle	*Gang*
alienated	*befremdet*
all of a sudden	*plötzlich*
amber	*Bernstein*
announcement	*Meldung*
an outburst of cursing	*ein Schwall von Flüchen*
anyone's guess	*reine Vermutung*
arm in arm	*eingehakt*
aromatic	*wohlriechend*
arrogant	*hochmütig*
as payback	*zum Ausgleich*
assess the situation	*die Situation einschätzen*
at breakneck speed	*mit einem Affentempo*
at full volume	*in voller Lautstärke*

at some unearthly hour	*in aller Herrgottsfrühe*
avalanche	*Lawine*
baa	*blöken*
back and forth	*hin und her*
baffled	*verwirrt*
bandana	*Kopftuch*
bar stools	*Barhocker*
barbecue	*Grill*
bark	*anbellen*
barn	*Scheune*
bashful	*schüchtern*
be beside oneself	*ganz aus dem Häuschen sein*
be claustrophobic	*Platzangst haben*
be honest	*ehrlich gesagt*
be in charge of	*für etw. verantwortlich sein*
be in favour of sth.	*für etw. sein*
be keen on	*scharf darauf sein*
be on one's heels	*jdm. dicht auf den Fersen sein*
be on the move	*unterwegs sein*
be spared	*verschont werden*
bed bugs	*Bettwanzen*
beg	*bitten*
bellow	*brüllen*
bewildered	*verdutzt*
big deal	*ein großes Geschäft*
bike rack	*Fahrradträger*
bikini beauty	*Strandschönheit*
bimbo	*Tussi*
blabber	*plappern*
blackmail sb.	*jdn. erpressen*

bless	*segnen*
blow your chances	*sich die Gelegenheit entgehen lassen*
boards	*Bretter*
body heat	*Körperwärme*
bog	*Sumpf*
bound to be	*werden müssen*
brain freeze	hier: *eingefrorenes Gehirn*
brat	*Balg*
bray	*wiehern*
breathlessly	*atemlos*
bridle	*Trense*
bring up the big guns	*schwere Geschütze auffahren*
bump into	*begegnen*
bump	*aneinanderstoßen*
bumpy	*uneben*
bundle of nerves	*Nervenbündel*
bureaucracy	*Bürokratie*
burst into fits of laughter	*in Lachkrämpfe ausbrechen*
bury	*einmauern*
but never mind that	*nun gut*
butcher	*Fleischer*
butt naked	*splitternackt*
by candlelight	*bei Kerzenlicht*
cackle	*gackern*
calm down	*sich beruhigen*
canoe	*Kanu*
carthorse	*Kaltblut*
catch a cold	*sich erkälten*
cauldron	*Kessel*
cement the bond	*das Band knüpfen*

certificate	*Bescheinigung*
chair lift	*Sessellift*
challenged	*behindert*
change of plan	*Planänderung*
change of tune	*Kehrtwendung*
change one's mind	*sich anders entschließen*
chaperone	*Begleiter*
cheat on sb.	*jdn. betrügen*
cheese dishes	*Käsegerichte*
chew	*kauen*
chilly	*kühl*
chivalrously	*ganz Kavalier*
chuck	*werfen*
chuckle	*glucksen*
clamour	*zetern*
clever clogs	*Schlauberger*
cling to	*aneinanderklammern*
clone	*Klon*
come to a decision	*einen Entschluss fassen*
compartment	*Abteil*
country bumpkin	*Landei*
cowpat	*Kuhfladen*
crack up with laughter	*herzhaft lachen*
crackle	*knistern*
crackling tile stove	*Kachelofen*
crafty	*schlau*
crash	*krachen*
crooked	*schief*
cross-country	*querfeldein*
crouch	*hocken*

cuddle	*Umarmung*
curse	*verfluchen*
dangerous stunts	*halsbrecherische Verrenkungen*
darting flame	*Stichflamme*
daydream	*Tagtraum*
debt	*Schuld*
deceive	*täuschen*
deckchair	*Liegestuhl*
delegation	*Delegation*
delicate physique	*zierliche Figur*
delude oneself	*sich täuschen*
descend on	*sich stürzen*
deserve	*verdienen*
despair at	*an etw. verzweifeln*
disapprovingly	*missbilligend*
doubtful	*zweifelhaft*
drag along	*jdn. mitreißen*
dressing gown	*Bademantel*
drip down	*abtropfen*
drive sb. up the wall	*jdm. auf den Wecker fallen*
drizzly	*nieselig*
drop back	*sich zurückfallen lassen*
dryly	*trocken*
dump	*abladen*
dyke	*Deich*
early riser	*Frühaufsteher*
edgy	*nervös*
enchanted	*verzaubert*
envy	*Neid*
eternity	*Ewigkeit*

exasperated	verärgert
exhausted	erschöpft
fabric softener	Weichspüler
fall for sth. hook, line and sinker	voll auf etw. hereinfallen
fall head over heels in love with	sich in jdn. verknallen
false enthusiasm	falsche Begeisterung
false nose	Pappnase
farm machinery	Landmaschinen
fate	Schicksal
feast on	schlemmen
feathered hat	Federhut
fence	Zaun
fire fuel	Brennpaste
firmly	bestimmt
first leg	erste Etappe
fish out	pfriemeln
flannel night gown	Flanellnachthemd
flash through my mind	mir durch den Kopf schießen
flat tyre	Reifenpanne
flatten	niederwalzen
flattering	schmeichelnd
flick through	durchblättern
flicker up	aufzüngeln
flimsy	labbrig
flock	Herde
flotsam and jetsam	Strandgut
foam	Schaum
foghorn	Nebelhorn
foist	unterschieben
for now	fürs Erste

forced labour	*Zwangsarbeit*
forced peck on the cheek	*Zwangsbussi*
freckles	*Sommersprossen*
from the other side	*aus dem Jenseits*
frown	*stirnrunzelnd ansehen*
gangway	*Laufsteg*
gasp	*keuchen*
gather oneself up	*sich aufraffen*
Geese	*Gänse*
get into one's head	*sich in den Kopf setzen*
get on your nerves	*nerven*
get rid of	*abwimmeln*
get tangled up	*sich verheddern*
get to the bottom of sth.	*aufklären, etw. auf den Grund gehen*
get your hands dirty	*sich die Hände schmutzig machen*
gifted	*begnadet*
give a compliment	*loben*
give sb. a shove	*jdn. schubsen*
give sb. a word of warning	*jdn. abmahnen*
give way	*nachgeben*
give your word	*sein Wort geben*
glance	*blicken*
glint	*Glitzern*
glumly	*mürrisch*
go deaf	*taub werden*
go on strike	*streiken*
gossip mag	*Klatschblatt*
growl	*knurren*
groyne	*Buhne*
grumble	*motzen*

guzzle	*schlürfen*
hammer	*schlagen*
hang around	*herumhängen*
hang on every word	*am jmds Lippen hängen*
hang up	*auflegen*
harbour	*Hafen*
haunt	*spuken*
have a screw loose	*ein Rad abhaben*
have enough	*die Nase voll haben*
have second thoughts	*sich etw. anders überlegen*
have to deal with	*herumplagen*
hearty	*herzhaft*
heatwave	*Hitzewelle*
hesitate	*zögern*
hidden from view	*vor Blicken geschützt*
high five	*jdn. abklatschen*
hilarious	*urkomisch*
hiss	*anzischen*
hit the sack	*ins Bett gehen*
hitch	*Haken*
hole	*Loch*
homely smell	*heimeliger Duft*
hoof	*Huf*
horribly unsocial habit	*schrecklich unsoziale Gewohnheit*
hula skirts	*Basträckchen*
hurry along	*zur Eile antreiben*
hustle	*scheuchen*
I get the impression	*ich habe den Eindruck*
illegal	*gesetzwidrig*
immerse	*tauchen*

impatient	*ungeduldig*
impressive	*beeindruckend*
in a nutshell	*kurz gesagt*
in astonishment	*verwundert*
in complete bewilderment	*verblüfft*
in high spirits	*gut drauf*
in mid-air	*mitten in der Luft*
in my head	*vor meinem inneren Auge*
in no time	*in null Komma nichts*
in the can	*im Kasten*
in the direction of	*in Richtung ...*
in the first place	*überhaupt*
in the meantime	*zwischendurch*
in the middle of nowhere	*wo sich Fuchs und Hase gute Nacht sagen*
in tow	*im Schlepptau*
in unison	*einstimmig*
in very high spirits	*in sehr aufgeräumter Stimmung*
inappropriate	*ungeeignet*
incomprehensible	*unbegreiflich*
ingenious	*erfinderisch*
injured	*verletzt*
inner tube	*Fahrradschlauch*
innocence	*Unschuld*
interrupt	*unterbrechen*
intricate	*aufwendig*
irritable	*gereizt*
it didn't go to plan	*es hat nicht geklappt*
items	*Beutestücke*
joint effort	*Gemeinschaftsarbeit*
keep a straight face	*ernst zu bleiben*

knock sb. over	*jdn. umhauen*
lap-dog	*Schoßhund*
late in the day	*spät*
lathered up	*eingeschäumt*
learn off by heart	*auswendig lernen*
lend	*ausleihen*
let alone	*geschweige denn*
let sb. down	*jdn. enttäuschen*
like a sheep being clipped	*wie ein Schaf bei der Schur*
linen cupboard	*Wäscheschrank*
liquid	*Flüssigkeit*
lively	*lebhaft*
liver sausage	*Leberwurst*
lose patience	*Geduld verlieren*
love dish	*Liebesspeise*
lovebirds	*Turteltauben*
low tide	*Ebbe*
low-key	*unauffällig*
luggage bearer	*Gepäckträger*
lurk	*lauern*
madwoman	*Verrückte*
magic word	*Zauberwort*
majestic	*erhaben*
make a fool of oneself	*sich lächerlich machen*
make out	*herausfinden*
manage	*schaffen*
material damage	*Sachschaden*
mean well	*gute Absichten haben*
melt into his arms	*in seinen Armen dahinschmelzen*
Member of Parliament	*Parlamentsabgeordneter*

mercilessly	*gnadenlos*
merge	*verschmelzen*
mermaid	*Meerjungfrau*
milk	*melken*
mischievous	*verschmitzt*
miss the boat	*eine Gelegenheit verpassen*
misty	*nebelig*
moan	*raunzen*
moment of weakness	*Anflug von Schwäche*
moor	*Heide*
more appropriate	*treffender*
muffled	*dumpf*
mumble	*murmeln*
nag	*nörgeln*
nappies	*Windeln*
needless to say	*natürlich*
negotiation	*Verhandlung*
nervous breakdown	*Nervenzusammenbruch*
nip down there	*runterfahren*
not be able to sleep a wink	*kein Auge zumachen*
not have the faintest idea	*keine blasse Ahnung haben*
of their own free will	*freiwillig*
off the beaten track	*weit ab vom Schuss*
on board	*an Bord*
on the slopes	*auf der Piste*
oncoming traffic	*entgegenkommender Verkehr*
open-air	*Freiluft-*
our horror	*zu unserem Entsetzen*
out of breath	*außer Atem*
out of the corner of my eye	*aus dem Augenwinkel*

out of the question	*es kommt nicht in Frage*
over the moon	*überglücklich*
over the top	*übertrieben*
overdue	*überfällig*
overjoyed	*überglücklich*
overwhelmed with joy	*vor Freude überwältigt*
P.E. teacher	*Sportlehrer*
pant	*nach Luft schnappen*
parents' evening	*Elternabend*
pay in instalments	*ratenweise bezahlen*
pedal	*strampeln*
peel off	*abziehen*
peel potatoes	*Kartoffeln schälen*
period	*Menstruation*
personal possessions	*persönliche Gegenstände*
pessimistic	*schwarzseherisch*
petals	*Blütenblätter*
phase of the moon	*Mondphase*
picture sth.	*sich etw. vorstellen*
placid	*gelassen*
pluck	*pflücken*
poke one's nose in	*seine Nase hineinstecken*
pomander	*Duftbeutel*
pot of gold	*Goldschatz*
pouring rain	*strömender Regen*
powers of persuasion	*Überzeugungskraft*
practical joke	*Schabernack*
prematurely	*frühzeitig*
pressure	*Druck*
presumably	*vermutlich*

property	*Grundstück*
pull someone's leg	*jdn. auf den Arm nehmen*
pull the rug from under you	*jdm. den Boden unter den Füßen weg-*
	ziehen
puppy dog eyes	*große Augen*
put on the backburner	*auf Eis legen*
put one's foot in it	*ins Fettnäpfchen treten*
put out	*löschen*
put up with	*ertragen*
puzzled	*verblüfft*
quarters	*Unterkunft*
questioning look	*fragender Blick*
rage	*toben*
rainbow	*Regenbogen*
ransacked	*geplündert*
rational self	*Vernunft-Ich*
rave	*schwärmen*
reassure sb.	*jdn. beruhigen*
reassuring	*beruhigend*
rebuff	*Abfuhr*
recognition	*Erkennung*
redecorate	*renovieren*
rep	*Animateur*
resigned to sth.	*sich mit etw. abgefunden haben*
revive spirits	*seine gute Laune erneuern*
right behind him	*sofort hinterher*
roam freely	*sich frei bewegen*
roaring laughter	*schallendes Gelächter*
rock-hard	*steinhart*
rummage	*wühlen*

runny nose	*Triefnase*
sabotage	*sabotieren*
saddle *(Nomen)*	*aufsatteln*
saddle *(Verb)*	*Sattel*
sane	*zurechnungsfähig*
saunter	*schlendern*
scenery	*Landschaft*
scenic route	*Aussichtsstraße*
scoff	*über etw. spotten*
scowl	*missmutig starren*
screech	*kreischen*
screeching tyres	*kreischende Reifen*
secretly	*unauffällig*
self-catering log cabin	*Selbstversorgerhütte*
self-pity	*Selbstmitleid*
sensitive spot	*empfindliche Stelle*
set no store by sth.	*keinen Wert auf etw. legen*
set sail	*lossegeln*
set	*fest werden*
settle down	*sich beruhigen*
settle	*abmachen*
shark	*Hai*
sharp bend	*Knick*
shattered	*erschöpft*
sheepishly	*kleinlaut*
shimmering	*flirrend*
shoot up	*hochschießen*
shortly afterwards	*kurz danach*
show-off	*Angeber*
shriek	*kreischen*

sink	*heruntergehen*
sip	*Schlückchen*
skid	*gleiten*
slam on the brakes	*plötzlich heftig bremsen*
slam	*zuschlagen*
slap in the face	*Schlag ins Gesicht*
slap	*jdn. ohrfeigen*
sledge	*Schlitten*
sleep like a log	*wie ein Murmeltier schlafen*
slimy	*glitschig*
slipper socks	*Hüttenschuhe*
slog your guts out	*schwer arbeiten*
smirk	*grinsen*
snarl	*Knurren*
sneak *(Verb)*	*schleichen*
sneak *(Nomen)*	*Schleicher*
snog	*knutschen*
snore	*schnarchen*
snug	*eng*
snuggle	*kuscheln*
soaking wet	*patschnass*
somewhat	*etwas*
sore	*schmerzhaft*
spare part	*Ersatzteil*
spill out	*fallen*
spin-the-bottle	*Flaschendrehen*
spit out	*fauchen*
splendid	*prächtig*
spurt	*spritzen*
squeak	*quietschen*

squeals	Schreie
squeeze in	quetschen
stagger	taumeln
stammer	drucksen
stand on guard	Schmiere stehen
stand out	besonders glänzen
steaming	dampfend
steed	Ross
sternly	ernst
stew	Eintopf
stick around	dableiben
stifled	erstickt
stipulation	Bedingung
stoke up	anheizen
stop in your tracks	aufhalten
storage space	Laderaum
straight away	sofort
straighten up again	wieder richten
stray	streunend
stream down	herunterströmen
strip off	etw. abstreifen
stroke a cheek	die Wange streicheln
stroll	schlendern
stroppy	unwirsch
stubborn	hartnäckig
stuff	stopfen
suffocate	ersticken
superstition	Aberglaube
suppress	unterdrücken
swallowed laughter	unterdrücktes Lachen

sweat	schwitzen
sweet talk	schmeicheln
swig	Schluck
swill	Gesöff
switch	Schalter
swoop down	herabschießen
sympathetically	mitfühlend
sympathy	Mitleid
take at face value	etwas für bare Münze nehmen
take pity on sb.	Mitleid mit jdm. haben
take up	belegen
taken aback	überrumpelt
talk into	überzeugen
tense	angespannt
tentatively	zögernd
that's a shame	das ist schade
thaw out	auftauen
the brightest	der Hellste
the coast is clear	die Luft is rein
the finish line	Ziellinie
the least I can do	das Geringste das ich tun kann
the neighbouring cabin	Nachbarhütte
throw a spanner in the works	Sand ins Getriebe streuen
ticket collector	Zugbegleiter
tickle my funny bone	mein Zwerchfell kitzeln
tight budget	knappes Budget
tight-lipped	verschlossen
time trial	Zeitfahren
tingle	Prickeln
tiptoe	(auf Zehenspitzen) schleichen

to and fro	*hin und her*
toboggan run	*Rodelbahn*
tone of voice	*Tonfall*
torch	*Fackel*
tortured	*gequält*
tremble	*schlottern*
tried and tested	*bewährt*
trot	*traben*
troubling	*belastend*
tuck in	*reinhauen*
tuck into	*verputzen*
turn sb. down	*jdn. abweisen*
twist around your little finger	*um den kleinen Finger wickeln*
two-faced	*falsch, heuchlerisch*
udders	*Euter*
unbearable	*unerträglich*
under her spell	*verhext*
undergrowth	*Gestrüpp*
unfold	*sich entfalten*
unimpressed	*wenig begeistert*
unmistakable	*unverwechselbar*
update	*modernisieren*
upside down	*verkehrt herum*
uptight	*verklemmt*
urgent	*dringend*
utter dismay	*völlige Bestürzung*
utter	*sprechen*
visibly shaken	*sichtlich erschüttert*
visitor's tax	*Kurtaxe*
vital	*unverzichtbar*

vocal chords	*Stimmbänder*
volunteer for	*sich freiwillig melden*
wager	*Wetteinsatz*
waistband	*Hosenbund*
weave	*sich durchschlängeln*
what do I care	*was ist mir das schnurzpiepegal*
what on earth?	*Was in aller Welt?*
whimper	*wimmern*
whine	*jammern*
whisper sweet nothings	*turteln*
whizz past	*vorbei flitzen*
whizz	*sausen*
wholeheartedly	*ernsthaft*
wilt	*verwelken*
win hands down	*mit links gewinnen*
wind up	*veräppeln*
wink at	*zuzwinkern*
winter wilderness	*Wintereinsamkeit*
with some resignation	*resigniert*
wobble	*schwabbeln*
wounded goat	*waidwunder Bock*
wrap my arms around him	*meine Arme um ihn schlingen*
wrapped up warm	*dick eingemummelt*
wring out	*auswringen*
yellow jersey	*gelbe Trikot*
yelp	*jaulen*
you must be joking	*das kann doch wohl nicht dein Ernst sein*
yuck	*igitt*

Summer Downpour and Holiday Amour

1. Crosswords

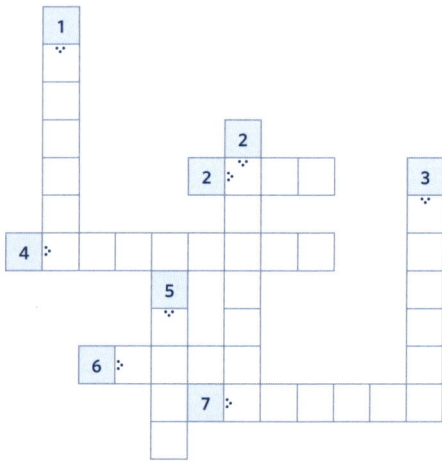

Across:

2. Spaß,

4. Sonnenschein,

6. Essen,

7. Sehenswürdigkeiten

Down:

1. Fotos,

2. Freunde,

3. Küsse,

5. Rundgang

2. Riding a bike

Kiki hat keine Ahnung, wenn es darum geht, ihr Fahrrad zu reparieren. Zum Glück hat sie ja aber Meik. Aber man lernt ja nie aus – auch bei Fahrradteilen nicht. Verbinde die Erklärung mit dem richtigen Wort.

1. You need them to stop.   ___ A tyre
2. You can carry your books in it.   ___ B handlebars
3. It covers the wheel.   ___ C gear
4. You hold onto them.   ___ D basket
5. It helps you go uphill.   ___ E brakes

3. Kiki's diary

Hier findest du ein paar Sätze aus Kikis Tagebuch, die durcheinander geraten sind. Kiki beschreibt ihre Gefühle vor, während und nach der Radtour. Schreibe die richtigen Gefühle in die Lücken und bringe dann die Sätze in die richtige Reihenfolge.

excited   jealous   proud   angry   confused

I now realise how silly I was. I am so _____ to be Meik's girlfriend.

This is really stupid, I can't believe my bike has broken down! I've never been so _____!

I feel so _____. I don't get it - why doesn't he want to snuggle up with me?

I can't wait to go to Mallorca again and chill out with the cute reps. I'm so _____!

Why did Franzi invite Mona? I'll admit that I'm already _____!

4. A holiday in the sun

Nach der Radtour schreibt Kiki eine Liste von Dingen, die sie für ihren Kurztrip nach Mallorca braucht. Was glaubst du, was Kiki alles einpackt? Schreibe 5 Dinge auf Englisch auf.

_____

5. Horse vocabulary

Mona ist Pferdeexpertin. Du auch? Übersetze folgende Wörter. Wenn du nicht weiterweißt, dann nimm ein Wörterbuch zu Hilfe oder schau nach unter www.pons.eu

1. hoof _____ **2.** tail _____ **3.** saddle _____

4. mane _____ **5.** lips _____

6. Weather words

In der Geschichte geht es oft ums Wetter. Gut, wenn du da ein paar Wettervokabeln parat hast. In der Wortschlange sind 8 Wörter zum Thema Wetter versteckt. Finde sie und schreibe sie neben die entsprechenden deutschen Übersetzungen.

ABOCCLOUDYGWYNHAILOONSTHUNDERPODUDRIZZLYMELSNOWYUNFALIGHTNINGXERSUNNYORAINY

1. sonnig _____

2. verschneit _____

3. Hagel _____

4. Donner _____

5. Blitz _____

6. regnerisch _____

7. nieselig _____

8. bewölkt _____

7. Scrambled sentences

In diesen Sätzen sind die Wörter durcheinandergekommen. Kannst du sie wieder in die richtige Reihenfolge bringen?

1. her dad/to stay/Kiki/in Berlin/with/wants

_____

2. catch/Kiki/they/the stray horses/Mona/tells/have to

_____

3. the cow/to milk/Greetje/unsuccessfully/tries

_____

4. Meik/a piece of amber/Kiki/his love/of/as a sign/gives

_____

8. Meik's birthday

Nach dem aufregenden Urlaub plant Kiki Meiks Geburtstag. Kannst du die Lücke mit dem richtigen Wort füllen?

> before because while
>
> until even though

1. Kiki wants to buy Meik a jumper _____ it is almost summer.

2. Kiki wants to throw Meik a big party _____ she knows he will enjoy dancing with his friends.

3. Kiki will keep buying Meik sweets _____ he says he doesn't want them anymore.

4. Kiki wants to organise the party _____ the end of the week.

5. Kiki is planning a suprise for Meik _____ he is at the football club.

9. I'm so cold!

Das Wetter auf der Radtour war wirklich grauenhaft und Kiki hat sehr darunter gelitten. Kannst du diese Wörter in die richtige Reihenfolge bringen – vom kältesten zum wärmsten?

> cold, toasty warm, chilly, just right, boiling hot, warm, hot, cool, freezing, frostbitten

\- _____ +

Hot Kisses, Cold Snow

1. Wordsnake

Katie ist ein großer Fan der Magie. In der Wortschlange sind 8 Wörter zu diesem Thema versteckt. Finde sie und schreibe sie neben die entsprechenden deutschen Übersetzungen. Benutze ein Wörterbuch, wenn du nicht weiterkommst.

1. Kessel _____

2. Zauber _____

3. Zauberspruch _____

4. Hexe _____

5. Geheimnis _____

6. Zauberstab _____

7. Besenstiel _____

8. Zaubertrank _____

2. Combine

Kannst du diese Ausdrücke richtig kombinieren? Als Hilfe findest du rechts die deutschen Übersetzungen. Kombiniere zuerst und verbinde dann mit den richtigen Übersetzungen.

Anders als im Deutschen, stellt man Vergleiche im Englischen mit **as ... as ...** an. Viele Vergleiche sind auch feste Redewendungen, die lernst du am besten als Ganzes.

1. as easy	A as an ox	taufrisch
2. as strong	B as mud	bärenstark
3. as free	C as silk	seidenglatt
4. as light	D as a bird	völlig unklar
5. as cold	E as ABC	eiskalt
6. as clear	F as a feather	federleicht
7. as fresh	G as ice	kinderleicht
8. as smooth	H as a daisy	frei wie ein Vogel

3. Scrambled letters

Katie muss ein paar Zauberwörter flüstern, um ihrer Liebesspeise Wirkung zu verleihen. Sie öffnet ihr Zauberbuch, aber leider sind die Buchstaben der Zauberwörter durcheinandergeraten. Kannst du sie wieder in die richtige Reihenfolge bringen?

1. ydeiorfnb _____

   Tip: Marcus is Mila's ...

2. mnocrae _____

   Tip: Is Vanessa looking for this with Kiwi?

3. srwpihe _____

   Tip: Marcus does this into Mila's ear.

4. guenlgs _____

   Tip: Mila enjoys doing this with Marcus.

5. sksi _____

   Tip: What Vanessa and Kiwi might do if the spell works.

4. Relax!

Eigentlich soll man im Urlaub ja entspannen, aber viele aus der Gruppe sind beunruhigt! Warum nur? Wer macht sich Gedanken um was? Setze die richtigen Namen in die Lücken.

1. _____is worried that Kiwi and Knolle will find her hiding in their room.

2. _____and_____ are worried that the hostel is haunted.

3. _____is worried that the teachers have eaten the love dish.

4. _____is worried that she might not be the quickest skier.

5. Skiing equipment

Hannah hat eine Liste geschrieben mit fünf Dingen, die sie beim Skiurlaub braucht. Leider kann sie die jetzt nicht finden! Schreibe eine neue Liste für sie. Mit einem Wörterbuch geht das ganz leicht!

6. Magic words

Hier findest du eine Seite aus Katies Zauberbuch. Ein paar Wörter sind in Geheimtinte geschrieben, damit sie nur von qualifizierten Hexen gelesen werden können.

Slowly   joyfully   carefully   warm

loudly   delicious   quietly

Recipe for Friendship Soup

1. _____ put the ingredients into the cauldron one by one.

2. Let it boil until it smells _____

3. Whisper the magic words _____

4. Dance around the cauldron _____

5. Shout the name of the person you want to be friends with _____

6. Count to ten as you stir the soup _____

7. Serve in a _____ bowl to your friend to be.

In den meisten Fällen werden aus Adjektiven Adverbien, indem ein **-ly** angehängt wird.

7. Writing a postcard

Marcus schickt eine Postkarte an seinen kleinen Bruder. Kannst du die korrekte Form des Verbs *to have* in die Lücken schreiben?

had ₕₐₛ **have** have **having** ₕₐᵥᵢₙg

Hey bro!

I 1 _____ to write a postcard to tell you how much fun I'm

2 _____! We 3 _____ been skiing every day and it 4 _____

been really cool learning to snowboard. You 5 _____ to come with me

next time!

Hope you're 6 _____ fun stuck at home ;p

Marcus.

8. The best word

Du siehst schon, die ganze Clique ist ziemlich oft mit ihren Handys beschäftigt. Unterstreiche in den folgenden Sätzen rund ums Thema Handy das passende Wort! Manchmal gibt es mehrere richtige Antworten!

1. I couldn't text you because my phone had run out of battery/time/credit.
2. I wanted to phone Hannah but there isn't a shop/signal/aerial here.
3. Everyone wants Vanessa's phone because it has a built in MP3 player/charger/camera.
4. I don't have to top-up my phone with credit because I have a pay-as-you go/new/contract phone.
5. The best thing about my mobile is that I can take photos/play games/listen to music on it.

9. Scrambled sentences

In diesen Sätzen sind die Wörter durcheinandergeraten. Bringe sie wieder in die richtige Reihenfolge.

1. Kiwi/a better skier/being/dreams of

_____

2. to play music/the girls/Marcus/with/wants

_____

3. is/with/Mila/not impressed/they/the celebrities/meet/in the village

_____

4. believed/Katie/wishes/in magic/her friends

_____

Summer Downpour and Holiday Amour

1. Crosswords
Across:
2. fun,
4. sunshine,
6. food,
7. sights
Down:
1. photos,
2. friends,
3. kisses,
5. tour

2. Riding a bike
1E, 2D, 3A, 4B, 5C

3. Kikis diary
1. proud, 2. angry, 3. confused, 4. excited, 5. jealous

4. A holiday in the sun
Sun hat, swimsuit, bikini, suncream, sunblock, book, passport, sunglasses, summer dress, flip flops, skirts, tops, lipbalm, money, phone, phrase book

5. Horse vocabulary
1. Huf, 2. Schwanz, 3. Sattel, 4. Mähne, 5. Maul

6. Weather words
1. sunny, 2. snowy, 3. hail, 4. thunder, 5. lightning, 6. rainy, 7. drizzly, 8. cloudy

7. Scrambled sentences
1. Kiki wants to stay with her Dad in Berlin.
2. Mona tells Kiki they have to catch the stray horses.
3. Greetje unsuccessfully tries to milk the cow.
4. Meik gives Kiki a piece of amber as a sign of his love.

8. Meik's birthday
1. even though, 2. because, 3. until, 4. before, 5. while

9. I'm so cold!
- frostbitten, freezing, cold, chilly, cool, just right, warm, toasty warm, hot, boiling hot +

. . . .

LOVE-QUESTIONS

1.
Nah babe, but ur not catching me out that easily! I
hate the rain! xxx

Kiki hat ihrem Freund schon vergeben, hat aber trotzdem immer noch keine Lust eine Radtour zu machen - auch wenn sie den Sommer mit Meik verbringen will.

2.
Yeah, I'm kinda excited
now. As long as it doesn't
rain! xx

Kiki gibt zu, sie freut sich jetzt darauf, die Radtour zu machen. Sie sorgt sich jedoch weiter um den Regen.

3.
Very soon! Can't w8
2 get back. Miss u,
xxx K

Kiki kann es auch kaum erwarten nach Hause zu fliegen. Obwohl sie zu Beginn unbedingt nach Mallorca wollte, kann sie der Insel dieses Jahr nichts abgewinnen, wo doch zu Hause Meik wartet. Aber die Liebe wächst ja mit der Entfernung!

Kisses in the Snow 💙

1. Wordsnake
1. cauldron, 2. magic, 3. spell, 4. witch, 5. secret, 6. wand, 7. broomstick, 8. potion

2. Combine
1E - kinderleicht, 2A – bärenstark, 3D – frei wie ein Vogel, 4F – federleicht,
5G – eiskalt, 6B – völlig unklar, 7H – taufrisch, 8C - seidenglatt

3. Scrambled letters
1. boyfriend, 2. romance, 3. whisper, 4. snuggle, 5. kiss

4. Relax!
1. Mila, 2. Kiwi and Knolle, 3. Katie, 4. Vanessa

5. Skiing equipment
Skis, jumper, jacket, bag, hat, goggles, socks, vest, gloves, scarf, snowboard, boots,
passport, lipbalm, book, money, phone

6. Magic words
1. Carefully, 2. delicious, 3. quietly, 4. joyfully, 5. loudly, 6. slowly, 7. warm

7. Writing a postcard
1. had, 2. having, 3. have, 4. has, 5. have, 6. having

8. The best word
1. battery/credit, 2. signal, 3. MP3 player/camera, 4. contract, 5. take photos/play
games/listen to music.

9. Scrambled sentences
1. Kiwi dreams of being a better skier.
2. Marcus wants to play music with the girls.
3. Mila is not impressed with the celebrities they meet in the village.
4. Katie wishes her friends believed in magic.

LOVE-QUESTIONS

```
1.
Everything OK — the boys
room is a mess :-) This is
all crazy and I hope it's
worth the pain! xxx
```

Kiki befindet sich mitten in der Höhle des Löwen und muss ein Kleidungsstück von Knolle entführen. Sie ist überzeugt davon, dass keine Magie der Welt Vanessa and Kiwi zusammenbringen wird und hofft, dass sich der ganze Aufwand lohnt.

```
2.
Ur crazy :-) ! U miss me so
much already?? I'll be with
you in a minute! XX K.
```

Kiki spottet über Marcus, da er ja nur ein paar Meter von ihr entfernt ist und ihr vor lauter Sehnsucht Nachrichten schickt. Aber insgeheim freut sie sich natürlich.

Freches Englisch mit den Frechen Mädchen